How *Not* To Miss God Moving

(Gospels Edition)

Craig A. Smith

Jeff & Peggy,
Dig deep & reach
Wide!

Shepherd Project Press

How Not To Miss God Moving (Gospels Edition)
Copyright © 2013 Craig Smith

Library of Congress Cataloging-in-Publication Data
Smith, Craig

> How Not To Miss God Moving / Craig Smith
> p. cm.
> Includes bibliographical references and indexes.
> ISBN-10: 0-9755135-7-5
> ISBN-13: 978-0-9755135-7-6

Shepherd Project Press
91 S. Carlton Street
Castle Rock, CO 80104
Email: info@shepherdproject.com

Contents

Chapter 1 - The God of Gracious Subtlety 7

The Great Adventure 8

To Catch A Wave 17

Windex for the Soul 19

What this Book Isn't and Is 25

Questions for Discussion 28

Chapter 2 - When Kingdoms Collide 31

Ruining Christmas 32

Unlikely Role Models 34

All Shook Up 44

Kings and Kingdoms in Conflict 50

Choosing Sides 54

Costly Choices 61

Questions for Discussion 64

Chapter 3 - Dealing with Doubt 67

Reluctant Doubters 69

Doubting Our Way to Faith 72

But Now I See 74

Understanding the Pharisees 89

A Matter of Focus 92

Faith and Logic 98

Questions for Discussion 100

Chapter 4 - Bitter **103**

A Very Thin Silence 104

Work vs. Worship 105

Too Busy to Be 106

Mary vs. Martha 116

The Slow Boil 118

The Poison of Bitterness 121

From Worship to Whining 123

The 80/20 Rule 126

Blinding Bitterness 128

Questions for Discussion 132

Chapter 5 - Too Happy to See **135**

Provision 138

Provider 146

The Bread of Life 151

Stomach or Soul? 154

Gifts and Givers 158

What's Your Basket? 162

Questions for Discussion 164

Chapter 6 - Conflicted Hearts **167**

Tragic Triumph 168

Cause for Concern 171

All the Usual Suspects 172

Stony Silence 174

Into the Robbers' Den 176

For All Nations 180

Stony Hearts 187

Misplaced Priorities 189

Heartbeats 191

Questions for Discussion 194

About The Author **200**

To Shane, who may not have succeeded in teaching me to surf, but who has inspired me to keep swimming hard after more important waves. Your growth as a man of God has been a joy to watch and your commitment to seek Him in all things is a constant, welcome challenge.

Chapter 1

The God of Gracious Subtlety

I entered pastoral ministry when I was 22. This was supposed to be a temporary thing, the briefest of sojourns… but my being allowed to think so was an act of grace.

As a child, I didn't dream of growing up to be a pastor. In fact, I can't remember ever giving it a single thought, but I'm certain that, if I had, it would not have been high on the list. Rather, like many pastors today, my journey into vocational ministry was a little bit like Barna's frog in the kettle: it caught me slowly and by surprise.

This was probably a good thing; if it hadn't happened so gradually, I would have probably run screaming in the other direction. Ignorance may or may not be bliss, but it is nearly always a mercy.

I'm not saying I had no idea what was happening. There were plenty of times along the way when I found myself asking suspiciously, "What's happening here?" But in the end, the realization that I was a pastor still came as a surprise. I can remember waking up once when I was about 30 and thinking to myself, "Am I really a pastor? How did that happen?"

The Great Adventure

Just in case you're wondering, my *first* plan for my life involved flying jet fighters, specifically the F-15. I grew up in an Air Force family and was obsessed with the F-15. How could I not be? It was very cool: loud, fast and capable of blowing all kinds of stuff into tiny bits. Who wouldn't want to be in charge of something like that? Unfortunately, I failed a vision test when I was in the fourth grade, and that was the end of that plan. Nowadays you can get your eyes re-shaped by lasers and still qualify to be a fighter pilot. But back then, plans of flying the F-15 could be pretty conclusively derailed by a school nurse with a messed-up alphabet chart.

My *second* plan was physics. I don't think it was a conscious thing, but I guess I figured, "Hey, if I have to wear glasses, I might as well go full-nerd." In this plan, I was going to work with a particle accelerator, taking tiny bits of matter and smashing them into even smaller bits. Now that I think about it, blowing things into tiny bits was a recurring theme of my early vocational planning.

I decided to modify this plan when I realized that I'm not really all that great at math and apparently this is a non-negotiable for physicists. Don't get me wrong: I'm pretty good at the whole *theory* of math, but the actual working out of real problems in order to get correct solutions...not really my thing.

In retrospect, I think what attracted me to physics in the first place might have been the theology of it: the workings of such an intricate, mind-bogglingly huge universe understood through the lens of simple, elegant principles that have God's fingerprints all over them. In any event, a year of high school calculus was enough to make me seriously reconsider the advisability of a career in quantum physics.

My *third* plan was rock star. Well, Christian rock star anyway, although I wouldn't have called it that if you had asked me back then. See, when I was eighteen I went on this retreat and had a very profound experience which led me to understand that God wanted me to be a Christian musician. That's probably an overly careful way to say it; the fact is I think God *told* me precisely that. You need to understand something right now, before we go any further together in this book: I don't use that kind of language lightly. For me to say, "God told me," something pretty dramatic has to have happened. In the course of my journey with God there have been only a tiny handful of experiences so unmistakable that I have felt comfortable using that kind of language to describe them. But, this was one of those few experiences.

What God had to say to me that day was a little surprising since I wasn't much of a musician at all back then, Christian or otherwise. However, a startling (one might even say *miraculous*) development of ability followed immediately after the experience, so I was pretty sure I now had a path and a plan.

And as I walked the path I understood God had led me to, He used me. I was singing in churches and at youth events and hearing from people who were genuinely touched by the music I was writing and performing, so I was confident that I'd finally understood God's will for my life.

To be sure, sometimes I had to do things that weren't really part of the plan: sometimes instead of just playing music at a youth retreat I had to serve as a counselor, and then someone talked me into actually putting together a leadership team and running a whole youth retreat, but on the whole the music thing seemed to be working out pretty well. Fortunately, I had met this amazing girl in college, Coletta Wetmore, who was really great at that planning and leadership development kind of thing. Working together we were able to take care of that non-music stuff with a minimum of disruption to my focus on my real calling:

music. So, as my college education was nearing its end, Coletta and I got engaged and began making plans to take a music team on staff with Campus Crusade for Christ.

The only problem was that we had to raise our own support, which takes time and, worse still, would delay us from doing the ministry we really wanted to be doing. But then God – who I have since learned can be pretty sneaky about this stuff – provided a great temporary solution: the man who discipled me in college told me that he had a friend who was leaving a youth pastor position at a church in Cincinnati. Would I be interested?

At first I really wasn't interested, but after some consideration, Coletta and I saw the advantages: we could do the job for a year, doing actual ministry with students and living on the salary from the church while we raised support in our free time! But after a year of full-time youth ministry, the plan changed: our hearts had been seized with a passion for evangelizing, teaching and discipling students in the context of a local church.

So, my *fourth* plan was youth pastor. We stayed at that church for three years (more on that later) and then, because we felt God's leading to do so, applied to Denver Seminary to study for an M.Div. with an emphasis in Youth & Family Ministry. We weren't entirely sure how we were going to pay for my education or a place to live or food to eat, but we were confident that we were obeying God's will, so we figured He would provide. When I summarize the process so succinctly it sure sounds spiritual, doesn't it?

We just sensed God moving and jumped on board! What could be simpler...or more faithful?

The reality was much messier, of course. And scarier. Much, much scarier.

It's one thing to sense God moving *into* your present circumstances...it's another thing entirely to sense God calling you *out of* your circumstances into unfamiliar, far countries.

I think our families thought we were young and foolish. I know my wife's family must have thought their daughter had hitched herself to a crazy boy. But to their credit and by the grace of God, both of our families were tremendously supportive – something for which we will always be grateful. I don't know that we would have ever made the move if they had tried to talk us out of it. While we might have appeared on the outside to be bold adventurers responding to God's call, on the inside we were terrified.

I would like to say that we had no doubts He would provide for us, but that wouldn't be true. I can remember saying things like, "Where God guides, He provides," but it took everything I had not to follow that proverb with the words "...at least I hope He will."

We had no idea how God would provide. The only thing we had was a clear sense that He was moving and a conviction that we needed to get on board.

But of course it's true: where God guides, He provides.

As soon as we arrived in Colorado, Coletta was offered a contract as a middle school teacher. I was hired as the youth pastor of a small church plant in Castle Rock, Colorado, just south of Denver. We were able to buy a small house, put some food in the kitchen pantry and set up shop in our new home.

Small churches can't usually afford one-trick-pony pastors, though, so they looked at my resume, noticed some references to music and asked if I would also serve as the church's worship pastor. I said sure, with a couple of stipulations: first, youth ministry was God's plan for my life, so that had to take priority; and second, I was more of a singer/songwriter than a worship leader, so while I would be happy to "fill in" as the worship pastor, we would need to find someone who was really "called" to that ministry as soon as possible.

Let's fast forward this a bit, shall we? That was almost 20 years ago and I'm still leading worship at that church. In the past two decades I've stepped out of worship ministry then stepped back in. I quit being a youth pastor at one point, then seven years later became an interim youth pastor again for a while. While I'm currently not a youth pastor, I continue to speak at youth conferences and train both students and youth pastors.

Far stranger, in the past twenty years, I've not only finished my M.Div., but also earned a Ph.D. in Biblical Studies from Bristol University in England and come back to serve as a professor at Denver Seminary, lecturing in both New Testament and Systematic Theology.

I've become part of a team called Shepherd Project Ministries that works nationally and internationally to equip Christians to maximize their impact on culture for the sake of Christ and his Kingdom. In that capacity I've gotten to speak and teach all over the world.

It's been a pretty busy 20 years.

Along the way, I've learned a thing or two about recognizing God's will for my life. Actually, let me rephrase that. See, I've pretty much given up trying to figure out what God wants me to do with my life, and started asking what I've come to realize is a much better question: what does God want me to do with my life *right now*?

And that simple, yet profound, shift in my thinking is at the heart of this book.

You see, the best parts of my life have not come from my plans, but from seeing God move and rushing to get on board.

I'm not saying that there's anything wrong with making plans. On the contrary, I think that John Ortberg is right: if you want to walk on water, you've got to get out of the boat.[1] I also fully echo Kevin DeYoung's challenge to "just do something."[2] God is all-powerful and doesn't need any help from us, but He chooses to invite our cooperation.

---

[1] John Ortberg, *If You Want to Walk on Water, You've Got to Get Out of the Boat* (Zondervan, 2001).
[2] Kevin DeYoung, *Just Do Something: A Liberating Approach to Finding God's Will* (Moody Publishers, 2009).

Given this divine choice to invite rather than to *force*, the reality is that human beings are much easier to guide if they're already moving.

When I say that the best parts of my life didn't come from my plans, I don't mean to suggest that my plans were a waste of time. They weren't, because God has used every one of them.

See, I can talk to people in the military because I know where they're coming from and because I share some of their passions. My love of physics has become a platform for speaking and writing in the field of Apologetics. My love of music lets me blend the head and the heart and opens doors for ministry in places where a theologian can't easily go. My work with students and youth pastors keeps me in tune with the ever-changing modern world. My interest in art and culture, combined with my education, allows me to bridge the gap between the ivory tower of academia and the muddy trenches of the modern world. All of this is good stuff and God has used it.

The problem wasn't the plans. Where I went wrong was in assuming that, when God moves in our lives, it's like a train that leaves Station A, travels straight along a rigid set of tracks and arrives predictably at Station B. I don't think that anymore.

What I think now is that God often nudges us to pack a suitcase and head down to the train station. There, we climb onto the platform expecting to catch one train when suddenly, across the station, we see Jesus beckoning from

15

the door of a railcar that's just about to depart. So, we race through the station and throw ourselves aboard just in time. Out of breath, we climb to our feet, dust ourselves off and ask, "So where's this train going?"

Sometimes, he answers. Sometimes he tells us, in one way or another, where the train is headed. But you know what I've found? Knowing were the train is going is rarely all that helpful. When I have been given a glimpse of where we were headed, the only thing I've ever been able to say in response is, "Oh…okay."

That's my new motto in life, by the way – the only one that actually says anything meaningful about what I have come to believe about a life lived pursuing God. Forget *carpe diem* or some other grand-sounding life mandate. My motto in life is just that: "Oh…okay." It's not profound, but it is honest. And in its own way, it's profoundly comforting.

Sometimes – *most* times, actually – when we ask where the train is headed, he doesn't answer. He just smiles and we eventually realize that's the most important answer.

Where the train is going doesn't really matter all that much. What matters is that he's going there…and that we are going there with him. Besides, the bag was already packed and we've got what we need

Where the train is going doesn't really matter all that much. What matters is that he's going there…and that we are going there with him.

for the journey...we're just headed somewhere we hadn't initially anticipated.

You know what they call that? An adventure.

To Catch A Wave

I don't necessarily mean to suggest that God is unpredictable, although I think that our inability to understand God in His fullness will always mean that He surprises us on a regular basis. He is not, as C.S. Lewis reminded us, a *tame* lion. But on some level, the more we come to know God the more we will be able to anticipate the kinds of things He is likely to do. Jesus himself said as much:

> *I no longer call you servants, because a servant does not know his master's business. Instead, I have called you friends for everything that I learned from my Father I have made known to you.*

> (John 15:15)

Our growing ability to anticipate the kinds of things God will do is not, however, the same as being able to predict the actual form those kinds of things will take. I am no longer surprised when God moves in a way I didn't expect. Well, that's not quite right. I am still surprised, which is probably a good thing. Perhaps I should just say that I am no longer surprised when God surprises me.

What I do think, however – what I know – is that *when God moves, we must move too.* If that requires a change in direction, so be it. If that requires a whole new plan, then toss out the old one and get cracking on the new one.

How God will move, where God will move…these are often unpredictable, not because God is capricious but because while God is a God of order, He is not a God of rules. Our job is not to assume or to predict but merely to recognize and respond. And that is what this book is all about: learning to recognize and respond when God moves.

You may have noticed that I haven't said much about what I call the "burning bush" experiences where God speaks so directly, so undeniably, that no one could possibly miss them. To be honest, I have had a couple of those in my life. My initial calling into music ministry was one of them, but here's the thing: the burning bush moments have always been the exception.

I have seen God move far more frequently in ways that are subtle enough to miss if we aren't looking – or are looking in the wrong places.

Do not make the mistake of assuming that such divine movements are less profound. If anything, the opposite is true. Sometimes the most powerful movements are first announced in ways that are easily missed.

I'm not a surfer, but I've given it a try a time or two. I like the *idea* of surfing, but I'm not very good at the practice of it. In addition to being physically intense, it's also psychologically frustrating. I can't tell you how many times I've thought a wave was going to be stronger than it actually was or thought that a little swell wasn't worth the energy it would take to catch.

But there is an important spiritual lesson I've learned while bobbing about in the ocean: the signs that mark the arrival of a great wave are often subtle at first, and easily missed. In fact, some of the best waves are at first discerned in a myriad of subtle changes in the waters that only experienced surfers know how to read. When such waves finally reveal themselves, and the fortunate pros are exuberantly sliding down their emerald faces, there are always a host of disappointed paddlers slapping the water in frustration and asking, "How did I miss that?"

In my journey with Christ these past decades I have rarely been alerted to God's movement by a burning bush experience, but I have often been alerted to His movement by subtle changes in the waters. Learning to read those shifts of current has enabled me to catch the wave of God's movement in exhilarating ways.

Windex for the Soul

We can miss God moving for a variety of reasons, some of them more obvious than others. This book is not really about these obvious things, but we have to give them some thought here at the beginning. There are certain obstacles to seeing God move that we have to make sure are not obscuring our vision before we go any further.

As I write these words, there's something wrong with the hood-release mechanism on my car. That wouldn't really be a problem except that the other day I ran out of windshield washer fluid. Since I can't get the hood to release, I can't get in there to add more fluid. I've been busy (read: lazy), so I didn't worry too much about it. I mean, the windshield was a little dirty, but it wasn't a big deal. Then I had to drive home after a snow storm. The roads were covered in slush that kept getting thrown onto my windshield, but that was fine...as long as it was wet enough, my windshield wipers kept the glass clear. But as the sun dried up the roads, less and less actual moisture made it onto my windshield. Eventually, the glass was coated in a dry grime that significantly affected visibility.

Still, I felt like I could see well enough to continue, so I just kept going. I made it back to town with no problems. I drove to my neighborhood without any difficulty. I turned down my road without a hitch...then drove right past my own house.

Now, in my defense, my house looks a lot like my neighbors' houses, one of the benefits of living in a covenant controlled community that strictly regulates what paint colors we can use. But still, I should have been able to spot my house, shouldn't I? But I couldn't, because the windshield that I thought was "clean enough" was actually so opaque that I couldn't make out enough details to spot my own home.

Similarly, there are some things that can blur our spiritual vision so much that we will have little or no hope of seeing God move, no matter how powerfully He might do so. We need to make sure these obstacles aren't obscuring our vision before we even bother to look at some of the more subtle things that are the primary concern of this book. Some of these obstacles we must address first include:

- **Absence of the Holy Spirit** – This book assumes that you are a born-again Christian; that is, that you believe that Jesus is the unique Son of God who lived a perfect life, died as a sacrifice for our sins and rose again after three days. This book assumes that you have personally trusted in Jesus' sacrifice on the cross for your forgiveness and have received the Holy Spirit who is both a deposit guaranteeing your salvation (Eph 1:13-14) and your guide in truth (John 16:13). Without the Holy Spirit you will not have the spiritual discernment necessary to see God move, and overcoming the obstacles discussed in this book will be impossible.

- **Unaddressed sin** – God doesn't require us to have achieved perfection before He moves in our lives. If that's what was required, then no one could ever experience the hurricane of God's grace that is salvation. But when we are mired in a habit of sin and unwilling to repent of it, we will often find ourselves blind to what God is doing around us.

- **Chronic biblical ignorance** – The Bible is not the only way in which God speaks, but it is the first and most important place where we come to know who He is and what He is like. This knowledge is critical to recognizing God when He moves.

- **Denial** – Human beings have an amazing capacity to tune out things they don't really want to hear or have to deal with. Unless we are willing to accept the fact that God may move us in ways we aren't necessarily excited about moving, we may find that we simply ignore the signs.

- **Apathy** – I find myself struggling with this every time I try to go surfing. After a while, the attention required to read the subtle shifts of current and get my board moving in time to catch the coming wave is just too much and I give up. I'd rather just lie on my board and let the wave pass me by than make the effort to catch it. The same thing can happen in our pursuit of God. We can get tired of the effort and just give up, settling into an apathetic lethargy that causes us to miss what God wants to do in and through us.

If you are struggling with any of these things, now is the time to deal with them. The rest of this book will be meaningless if you don't – like asking for directions to someplace when you're handcuffed to a lamppost.

If you cannot say with confidence that you are a born-again Christian, then what's stopping you from trusting in Jesus as your Savior right now? If the answer is something like, "I don't really know what I believe about Jesus," or "I have some big, unanswered questions," then find a Christian to talk to, someone who can help you find the answers you need. If the answer is simply, "I've just never made that commitment," then why not do it right now? Just say to God, "I'm sorry for my sins. Thank you for sending your own Son to offer me forgiveness. Jesus, thank you for dying in my place. Please take away the eternal consequences of my sin and take your place as Lord and Savior in my life. Holy Spirit, please come to me and mark me for salvation by living in me. Give me the spiritual eyes to see God moving in my life."

If you're a Christian, but know of unaddressed sin in your life, repent of it (which means commit to turning away from it), confess it to God and accept His forgiveness.

> *If we confess our sins, he is faithful and just and will forgive us our sins and purify us from all unrighteousness.*
>
> (1 John 1:9)

If you realize that you don't know enough about who God is and what He is like to recognize Him even if He did move in your life, get involved in a church that works hard to teach the Bible. Get involved in a small group Bible study. And above all else, start reading the Bible!

If, after careful reflection, you find yourself having to admit that you've got a problem with denial, then that may be a little trickier. For many people, this kind of denial emerges only after they've already begun to sense that God is moving them towards something scary – or away from something comfortable. My advice is that you ask God through the Holy Spirit to show you which one it is and then ask for a renewed faith to deal with it. In any event, it will probably be very helpful to share your struggle with a trusted Christian friend, pastor or counselor.

If you feel like you're struggling with apathy, feeling like you're just too tired to care, that you'd rather miss God move than make the effort to catch the wave, then realize that's probably not true. If you had really given up, why would you be reading a book like this?

There's a profound difference between struggling with feeling like you just can't push on in your pursuit of God and giving in to a settled apathy. If there is even a glimmer of desire to see God move in your life, then chances are that you are weary rather than truly apathetic. And chances are also good that you're weary because you've been swimming against the current rather than with it, fighting to catch a wave by your own strength rather than discerning how to get on board with what God is doing. If you're exhausted, but not truly apathetic, then read on. This book may be a subtle grace, something God brings into your life to help you identify the blinders that have prevented you from seeing all that He longs to do in you.

These obvious things are not the subject of this book. It doesn't take a theologian or a Bible scholar to know that unaddressed sin or chronic apathy will get in the way of our seeing God move. But we may also miss God moving for other, more subtle reasons – ones that we may be far less prepared to identify on our own.

This book is about understanding *those* things and identifying them in us so that we can begin cooperating with the Holy Spirit to remove their blinding influence from our lives.

What this Book Isn't and Is

Understand, this book is not a step-by-step guide to discerning God's will for your life – or even for your life right now. This book is not about how to pick God's voice out of the crowd. Those are important issues, but they are, to some degree, secondary ones.

When I walk into a crowded room where my bride is talking to someone, I can pick out her voice very quickly. The main reason for that is simply that I have spent a lot of time listening to her over the years. I know what her voice sounds like; I know the timbres and the pitches, the cadences and the inflections.

Those are all important things to know, but if I had cotton in my ears, those things would make no difference at all. Knowing what Coletta's voice sounds like won't matter if there is something that will keep me from hearing it in the first place.

It's the same way with God. If we want to hear God speak, to detect the subtle changes in current that signal a spiritual swell, to catch sight of him beckoning from a soon-to-depart train…if we want to see God *move*, we first have to make sure we're not doing the things that will make us blind and deaf to such movement.

In short, we have to know how not to miss God moving.

That's what this book is about.

The approach will be very simple. Each of the next several chapters is essentially a Bible study based on a series of passages from the Gospels. I've chosen each of these passages because they describe two different individuals or two different groups of people. In each case, one of those individuals or groups recognized God moving and caught the wave. The other group missed it.

Our focus will be primarily on what the Bible seems to reveal about those individuals or groups who missed God moving. I have chosen this somewhat odd approach for a simple reason: every time I read about these people who didn't see what God was doing, I find myself asking, "How could they miss it?" And when I read more carefully and come to understand what made them miss it – miss Him – I also realize that I often have the same blinders on. When I am able to identify what made *them* miss God moving, I am also able to see what role that thing is currently playing in *my* life, and take steps to remove its influence.

My hope is that you will find yourself able to do the same thing and, by doing so, learn how not to miss God moving.

Questions for Discussion

1. *When you were a child, what did you most want to be when you grew up? Has God fulfilled that desire or used it in some other way?*

2. *Is the idea of God moving in your life right now more exhilarating or terrifying? Why?*

3. *On a scale of 1-10, with 1 being "I hope He doesn't" and 10 being "I'm desperate for Him to," how ready are you to see God move in your life?*

I hope
He doesn't
move

I'm desperate
for Him to
move

4. *What factors contribute to how ready/not-ready you are to see God move?*

5. *As was mentioned in this chapter, there are some obvious obstacles that keep us from seeing God move: things like sin, ignorance, denial and apathy. Do you feel that you have a significant struggle with one of those things?*

Chapter 2

When Kingdoms Collide

If you had asked me twenty years ago what God's plan for my life was, it would never have occurred to me that it might involve lecturing at a seminary. However, not only has that become an important part of the ministry God has called me to, it has become one of the most rewarding. I love being able to work with men and women preparing for a lifetime of effective Christian ministry.

I know that some people view the world of academic Christianity with suspicion. I've heard all the jokes. My favorite one is, "Oh, you teach at a cemetery…oops, sorry, *seminary*?" And I understand that what they're reacting against is the idea that authentic Christian faith can be reduced to factual knowledge about God. It can't. But, authentic, vibrant Christian faith is incompatible with ignorance.

Understanding and articulating Christian truth in the real world requires a robust knowledge of what the Bible teaches and a careful consideration of how this truth plays out in contemporary life and culture. This integration of doctrinal understanding and cultural adeptness doesn't just happen without careful training, and that's what a good seminary works hard at to provide. And that's what I love about teaching at a seminary: I get to help students dig deep and reach wide.

Ruining Christmas

One of my favorite classes to teach is called *Understanding the Gospel and Acts*. Every semester that I get to teach this course, I do a little Christmas exercise. It's pretty simple really: I break all the students into small groups and hand each group a couple of sheets of paper containing the lyrics to some popular Christmas hymns. Their job is to take all the statements in the lyrics and fact-check them against the Gospel accounts.

My students call it "Ruining Christmas."

When it comes to factual accuracy, some songs fare better than others. However, nearly every Christmas song you've ever heard has some statements in it that cannot be easily supported by evidence from Scripture.

I'm not saying that the hymns lie or distort the truth, because, for the most part, the questionable statements are just artistic license. However, when we look at the biblical accounts of Jesus' birth carefully, we come to realize how much our mental pictures of that first Christmas actually depend on such artistic license rather than on historical fact.

I would venture to say that the average Christian's conception of the first Noel is rooted more in popular songs than in biblical truth.

Where most of the songs run afoul of our fact-checking is in the extraneous details they add to the scene. Usually these are innocent and innocuous, but sometimes, in the attempt to convey some transcendent aspect of the moment, they miss the point entirely. Every semester, someone ends up asking about this line from Silent Night: *radiant beams from thy holy face.*

"Why did they think that baby Jesus was glowing?" is usually what students want to know.

Another line that comes under scrutiny every semester is the one that says "no crying he makes."

You know, I'm sure Mary was pretty stressed out by the whole thing already: a pregnant virgin giving birth to a baby in a cattle stall. Now, to top it off, the baby was eerily silent…and glowing, of course!

What the song is trying to do is signify the *otherness* of Jesus from the moment of his birth, portraying him as unlike other infants. On one hand, I can appreciate this. The very fact of the Virgin Birth means that Jesus was born without a sin nature[3] and in that sense he is unlike any other human being who has ever been born since the Fall. But the problem is that this attempt to make baby Jesus so *other* misses the entire point of the Incarnation, which is that the Son of God became one *with us* by becoming one *of us*. He was a real human being and, as such, he was every bit as frail and frightened as any other human infant. Surely he cried when he first pulled air into those fresh pink lungs.

But I digress.

Unlikely Role Models

As I work through this exercise with my students, I am always intrigued by another place where the Christmas carols diverge from the biblical evidence: the so-called

---

[3] Theological Excursion: According to Scripture, we inherit the sin nature from our human father (1Co 15:22). Some theologians, myself included, think that the seed of the human soul is passed from parent to child, similar to the way that the seed of the human body is passed, a view known as Traducianism. In the same way that there are sex-linked genetic traits that can only be passed from the mother or the father to their offspring, there may be spiritual traits that can only be passed by one parent, one of which is the sin nature which can only be transmitted by the father. Mary herself would have had the sin nature since she had received it from her own father, Heli, but if this particular spiritual trait is only transmitted by the father, then the lack of a human father would explain why Jesus was born without the sin nature.

"wise men." First, as my students quickly note, the Bible doesn't say there were three of them. In fact, the Bible doesn't give any indication of how many there were at all. My guess is that we have assumed there were three because there are three gifts mentioned (gold, frankincense and myrrh), but that's sketchy evidence for a tradition that has become "fact" for most Christians today.

Much more important than how many there were, however, is the way these songs refer to these individuals. Consider:

> *We three kings of Orient are*
> *Bearing gifts we traverse afar*
> *Field and fountain, moor and mountain*
> *Following yonder star*

Why do we think they were kings?

Well, there are a few things which might explain this perception. First, they were obviously wealthy. The gifts they brought were expensive and beyond the reach of the common person, so unless they were wildly successful merchants, they probably had some kind of connections to royalty. Second, they obviously had a fair amount of free time. Think about it: they spent a lot of time gazing at stars and traversing afar. Neither of those were things that the average person had time for. Again, people who had that kind of free time were usually connected in some way to royal families.

On the other hand, actual kings probably wouldn't have been doing what these individuals did either. Kings wouldn't have been able to make an extended journey like this and they almost certainly wouldn't have come to do what these men said publically they were there for: *we have come to worship him* (Mat 2:2).

So, while it seems likely that they had some kind of connection to royalty, it also seems likely that they weren't actually kings. Recognizing this, we sometimes prefer to call them "wise men" which is at least closer to the truth, but we need to recognize that neither the term "king" nor "wise man" is found in the biblical description.

The Gospel of Matthew, which is the only one who mentions them, uses the term *magos*. This is probably a Persian loan-word used to refer to people who practiced astrology (reading the stars for signs of what the future holds) and a host of other occult activities. The same term was used in the book of Daniel to refer to "magicians" that served Nebuchadnezzar (Dan 2:2, 2:10)[4] and in Acts to refer to a magician names Elymas (Acts 13:6, 13:8). Typically these were individuals who served as advisors to kings and other rulers, which explains the royal connections noted above.

So let's be clear: the Magi were most likely pagan magicians. And when I say "magicians," I'm not talking about the guys you can find on the Vegas Strip. The Magi

---

[4] This portion of Daniel was originally written in Hebrew, but an ancient Greek translation of the Old Testament known as the Septuagint (sometimes referred to as the LXX) uses the term *magos* to translate the Hebrew *ashaph* which means "conjuror" or possibly even "necromancer."

had far more in common with shamans, mediums, psychics and witches. Think Voldemort rather than David Copperfield.

So why have we opted to call them kings or wise men rather than what the Bible calls them? I imagine it's because we are uncomfortable with the idea of occultists being featured positively in a biblical story. After all, the Bible has some pretty serious warnings about such people:

> *Let no one be found among you who sacrifices his son or daughter in the fire, who practices divination or sorcery, interprets omens, engages in witchcraft, or casts spells, or who is a medium or spiritist or who consults the dead. Anyone who does these things is detestable to the LORD, and because of these detestable practices the LORD your God will drive out those nations before you.*

> (Deuteronomy 18:10-12)

> *Manasseh was twelve years old when he became king, and he reigned in Jerusalem fifty-five years. He did evil in the eyes of the LORD, following the detestable practices of the nations the LORD had driven out before the Israelites. He rebuilt the high places his father Hezekiah had demolished; he also erected altars to the Baals and made Asherah poles. He bowed down to all the*

37

starry hosts and worshiped them. He built altars in the temple of the LORD, of which the LORD had said, "My Name will remain in Jerusalem forever." In both courts of the temple of the LORD, he built altars to all the starry hosts. He sacrificed his sons in the fire in the Valley of Ben Hinnom, practiced sorcery, divination and witchcraft, and consulted mediums and spiritists. He did much evil in the eyes of the LORD, provoking him to anger.

(2 Chronicles 33:1-6)

The acts of the sinful nature are obvious: sexual immorality, impurity and debauchery; idolatry and witchcraft; hatred, discord, jealousy, fits of rage, selfish ambition, dissensions, factions and envy; drunkenness, orgies, and the like. I warn you, as I did before, that those who live like this will not inherit the kingdom of God.

(Galatians 5:19-21)

Obviously, this sort of stuff is bad business and it was strictly forbidden among God's people. So how can these occultists show up in the Gospel of Matthew as role models?

When I say they were role models, I'm saying that they did the right thing, the thing God's people were supposed to be doing. Let's face it: regardless of how uncomfortable we might be with their real occupation, the Magi are treated very positively in Matthew's account of the birth of Jesus. Consider the evidence:

- The Magi recognized the cosmic significance of Jesus' birth, seeing that the heavens themselves chronicled it.
- The Magi brought royal gifts to welcome the birth of a king. All three gifts named were closely associated with royalty in the Ancient Near East.
- The Magi came to offer their respect to this new-born king. Literally, Matthew says that they came to "worship" him.
- The Magi obeyed God rather than Herod by following God's command to return by a different route, leaving Herod hanging.

There can be no doubt that the Magi are positive examples in Matthew. They saw God moving and they got on board.

Now, to understand the Magi in context, we must recognize that this surprisingly positive presentation of the Magi is part of a larger theme here in the early chapters of Matthew's Gospel: the theme of presenting Jesus as greater than Moses.

The Gospel of Matthew was originally written to a Jewish audience, probably one comprised of Jewish believers who had just been, or were in the process of being, forced out of their Jewish synagogues because of their faith in Jesus. Matthew was written, in part, to encourage these early

Christians that their faith was well-founded – encouragement that was sorely needed because of the severe hardships they were facing as a result of this faith.

For a first century Jew, Moses was the greatest possible example of God's provision for His people. Moses was the one God used to set Israel free from slavery in Egypt. Moses was the one who led the people through their forty years in the desert. Moses was the one who received the Law on Mount Sinai. You get the picture: Moses was the best.

But what Matthew did throughout his Gospel was demonstrate that, as great as Moses was, Jesus is better. The Gospel of Matthew continually does this by pointing to clear parallels between Moses and Jesus. Consider:

As an infant, Moses had to be protected from a king who wanted all the baby boys killed.	As an infant, Jesus had to be protected from a king who wanted all the baby boys killed (Mat 2:13-18).
Moses was born in Egypt.	Jesus' family fled to Egypt (Mat 2:13-18).
Moses spent 40 years in the desert.	Jesus spent 40 days and nights in the desert (Mat 4:2).

Moses met with God on a mountaintop (Sinai) where God spoke to him.	Jesus met with Moses and Elijah on a mountaintop where God spoke, telling them to listen to Jesus (Mat 17:1-5).
Moses received the Law.	Jesus said that he had come to "fulfill" the Law (Mat 5:17).
Moses received the Law on a mountain.	Jesus explained the Law on a mountain in a famous sermon called the "Sermon on the Mount" (Mat 5:1-7:29).
Moses had an encounter with pagan magicians.	Jesus had an encounter with pagan magicians (Mat 2:1-13).

The list of parallels can go on for a while still, but it's this last one that really interests us here, because it so clearly illustrates Jesus' superiority over Moses. While Moses fought and eventually defeated the Egyptian magicians, Jesus' encounter with the Magi was fundamentally different: we are told that they *worshipped* Jesus.

Now, the Greek term used in Mat 2:2 and translated as "worship" (*proskuneō*) doesn't necessarily mean religious adoration as the English suggests. Literally, it denotes the act of bowing down before someone or something. It certainly can be used of worshipping God in the religious sense, but it can also be used of bowing down before a human king.

In this particular case it doesn't necessarily indicate that the Magi recognized Jesus as God. What it does mean is that they were publically acknowledging the infant Jesus as someone who was greater than they. By the way, this is another piece of evidence to suggest that the Magi weren't actually kings themselves. It's hard to imagine actual kings from Persia travelling together at all, let alone coming together to acknowledge their inferiority to a foreign king to whom they owed no allegiance. However, it wouldn't be at all surprising for a king's advisors to be sent to offer gifts to another king before whom the advisors would bow down, acknowledging their lower status.

In Exodus, the Egyptian magicians were finally forced to admit that Moses had God on his side. When they failed to duplicate the plague of gnats, they told Pharaoh, "This is the finger of God" (Exo 8:18) *but they never bowed.* They never submitted to Moses or to the God who stood behind him. The Magi in Matthew, however, came to Jesus with the primary purpose of humbling themselves before him.

In this way, the story of the Magi furthers Matthew's purpose of demonstrating that Jesus is superior to Moses, and he retold it, in part, to help Jewish believers who were struggling with whether or not to remain loyal to Jesus in the face of persecution from other Jews who rejected Jesus.

There is another purpose to the story of the Magi as well. If you've spent much time in missions-minded churches, you're probably familiar with another famous text from Matthew's Gospel, known as the Great Commission:

> *Then Jesus came to them and said, "All authority in heaven and on earth has been given to me. Therefore go and make disciples of all nations, baptizing them in the name of the Father and of the Son and of the Holy Spirit, and teaching them to obey everything I have commanded you. And surely I am with you always, to the very end of the age."*

(Matthew 28:18-20)

For our purposes here, the interesting thing about the Great Commission is that it specifically instructs the followers of Jesus to go out into "all the nations," language that probably goes back to Gen 12 where God told Abraham:

> *"I will make you into a great nation and I will bless you; I will make your name great, and you will be a blessing. I will bless those who bless you, and whoever curses you I will curse; and all peoples on earth will be blessed through you."*

(Genesis 12:2-3)

In other words, Jesus is the fulfillment of God's promise to Abraham that through Abraham's line, all nations/peoples would be blessed. For the Jewish people, anyone who wasn't Jewish was called a Gentile, a word meaning something like "one from a foreign nation/people." Is it coincidence that a Gospel which *ends* with this statement of God's desire to take the good news to the Gentiles also *begins* with a story of how Gentiles responded positively to Jesus? Of course not. The story of the Magi foreshadows the giving of the Great Commission.

When we understand all this, the positive treatment of the Magi in the Gospel of Matthew isn't quite so hard to understand.

Matthew isn't condoning occultism. He's simply pointing out that some people who shouldn't have been expected to respond positively to God's moving *did* respond positively. And in that respect only, the Magi were unlikely role models for God's people.

All Shook Up

On the other hand, in the midst of the story of the Magi we also find illustration of the truth that sometimes the people we would most naturally expect to respond positively to God's moving don't:

> *After Jesus was born in Bethlehem in Judea,*
> *during the time of King Herod, Magi from*
> *the east came to Jerusalem and asked,*
> *"Where is the one who has been born king of*

the Jews? We saw his star in the east and have come to worship him." When King Herod heard this he was disturbed, and all Jerusalem with him.

(Matthew 2:1-3)

It's no surprise that Herod was disturbed.

How could he not be? It would have been fine if the newborn king was a child of his, as the Magi obviously expected him to be: isn't that why they had come to Jerusalem in the first place? They had seen a sign in the heavens that a king had been born in Israel. Herod was the king of Israel at that time. So, putting two and two together, they probably figured that a son had just been born to Herod.

Of course, if they had known anything about Herod, this would have been an unlikely scenario as he was almost 70 years old by this time and had already had several sons. On the other hand, Herod had executed three of his own sons just a few years previously and had recently taken a new wife, so perhaps the Magi thought he had sired a new successor by his most recent bride.

In any event, when the Magi arrived to congratulate him, Herod was immediately alarmed because he knew that there was no newborn king in his household. For obvious reasons, news of a king born outside his own family sent Herod into a paranoid rage.

So it makes sense that Herod was disturbed.

What is less understandable, however, is the widespread agitation implied by the simple words "and all Jerusalem with him" (Mat 2:3). Matthew is telling us that Herod was not the only one disturbed by the birth of this new king. Beyond the understandable upset of Herod and his house, the general populace of Jerusalem was also…well, what were they?

The Greek word here is *tarassō* which literally means something like "stirred up" or "shaken up." Matthew used this term only one other time in his Gospel, where it describes the reaction of the disciples when they saw Jesus walking on the water and didn't know who it was:

> *When the disciples saw him walking on the lake, they were <u>terrified</u>. "It's a ghost," they said, and cried out in fear.*

> (Matthew 14:26)

Here *tarassō* is translated as "terrified." Unfortunately, only two instances does not provide us with a solid foundation from which to understand any particular nuances that Matthew may have been communicating by this term, but the general sense is still clear: this word indicates a strong negative emotional reaction closely associated with fear.

However, this is not the normal word for simple fear. Typically, when Matthew speaks of someone being afraid, he uses the term *phobeō* (cf. Mat 1:20, 2:22, 14:27, etc.; this is the word from which we get *phobia*). *Tarassō* on the other hand, seems to imply something about the emotional turmoil that accompanies fear. Interestingly, it is used in the Gospel of John to describe the waters of the pool of Bethesda being "stirred up" (John 5:7). The overall sense of the word, then, is of someone being deeply unsettled, fearful even, unsure of what to do.

As we've already said, it is perfectly understandable that Herod should have felt this way when he received word that a king had been born in Israel. But why did all of Jerusalem share his emotional turmoil?

Interestingly, this is not the only account of Jerusalem being all stirred up on account of Jesus. A suspiciously similar description is given of the city at Jesus' triumphal entry into it near the end of his public ministry: *When He had entered Jerusalem, all the city was stirred, saying, "Who is this?"* (Mat 21:10). The word here translated as "stirred" is not the same one used in Mat 2:3, but it is very closely related.[5]

So the city that was in emotional turmoil at the *birth* of this king was the same city that was in emotional turmoil at this king's entrance into the city some 30 years later. Matthew

---

[5] The Greek term in Mat 21:10 is *seiō* which Louw & Nida (authors of a standard scholarly lexicon) group together with *tarassō* as belonging to the same semantic domain of things related to non-linear movement. Both *seiō* and *tarassō* are used in Matthew to describe emotional turmoil (cf. Mat 28:4).

is again pointing out how events during the beginning of Jesus' life foreshadow events from the end of it.

But this still doesn't really answer the question of *why* Jerusalem was so stirred up. If anything, the fact that it happened twice only increases our need to know.

It's also important to understand that "Jerusalem" here refers to more than just the physical city. While the Gospel of Matthew does include simple references to Jerusalem as a city (cf. Mat 4:25, 15:1, etc.), at other times it uses the name to signify something more significant. Following Jesus' own pattern, some verses in the Gospel of Matthew use Jerusalem to represent the entire Jewish nation. Consider:

> *"O Jerusalem, Jerusalem, you who kill the prophets and stone those sent to you, how often I have longed to gather your children together, as a hen gathers her chicks under her wings, but you were not willing."*

(Matthew 23:37)

As anyone familiar with the Old Testament history of Israel knows, the people of Jerusalem were not the only Israelites who mistreated God's prophets. But, as the capital of Israel and center of its worship in the first century, Jerusalem served as a kind of symbolic representation of the Jewish people as a whole and it is used in this way at various points by Jesus generally[6] and in the Gospel of Matthew particularly.

When Matthew tells us that Herod was disturbed "and all Jerusalem with him," he is likely saying more than just that the inhabitants of the city were disturbed. It is very likely that he is actually saying that Herod was disturbed *and all the Jewish people with him*. But again, why? The question just keeps getting more significant, but is there any answer to it?

I believe there is, and I think it's to be found in the rest of the quote from Jesus in Mat 23:

> *"O Jerusalem, Jerusalem, you who kill the prophets and stone those sent to you, how often I have longed to gather your children together, as a hen gathers her chicks under her wings, but you were not willing. Look, your house is left to you desolate. For I tell you, you will not see me again until you say, 'Blessed is he who comes in the name of the Lord.'"*

Did you catch it? The reason that Jerusalem – and the nation of Israel that it represented – would be left desolate was that they were not ready to be gathered "*as a hen gathers her chicks.*" They were not ready to say, "*Blessed is he who comes in the name of the Lord.*"

---

[6] For other examples outside the Gospel of Matthew, cf. Luke 2:38 and 13:34.

But does that really answer the question of why they were so disturbed at Jesus' coming? I think it does. You see, when they heard about the signs from the Magi, and later when they heard about the miracles of Jesus, they must have begun to wonder, "Could it be...? Is this...?" In short, they began to suspect that God might be moving; that their true King might be coming.

But here's the thing: *the people of Israel weren't kingless.* They already had a king: Herod, a tyrant of legendary brutality, a man who didn't hesitate to execute even his own children if he suspected they had rebellion in their hearts. To acknowledge Jesus as king necessarily meant denying Herod's kingship, something that no one would do lightly.

And Herod wasn't exactly a solitary sovereign. His rule was approved and enforced by the might of the Roman Empire. Saying, "Blessed is he who comes in the name of the Lord" would have meant that they were also saying to Herod and to all of Rome who stood behind him, "...and you guys can take a long walk off a short pier."

Kings and Kingdoms in Conflict

In short, the people of Israel knew that if God was moving, then kingdoms were about to collide. And they also knew that if kingdoms were about to collide, then they were going to have to choose sides.

That is why all Jerusalem was shaken up by the Magi's announcement that they had seen the signs, signs that suggested very strongly that God might be moving: the people of Jerusalem knew that when God moves, kingdoms collide, and *when kingdoms collide, we have to choose sides.*

Of course, when God's people are faced with a black and white choice between siding with God or with men, the choice is clear. We might lack the strength of character or conviction to *do* what is right, but it's not hard to *know* what is right when confronted with a clear choice between God and anything else. However, thankfully, the alternatives are usually not that stark. We are rarely forced to choose between God and not-God, but between two or more options where the rightness – the righteousness – of the options is not so obvious. In many ways, we prefer this ambiguity because it allows us to go with the flow and convince ourselves that we aren't doing anything wrong.

See, if we can't say conclusively that the status quo is wrong, then we can keep doing what we've been doing and not have to deal with all the unpleasant consequences of fighting against the current. And of course – or so we tell ourselves – if God were to show up and tell us plainly that we needed to do something different, then we wouldn't hesitate to do whatever He required. But since it's not really *certain* that He wants something different from us, we're content – relieved even – to keep on going the way we've been going, the way everyone else is going.

The problem with this kind of thinking, of course, is that it means that when we begin to suspect that God might be moving us to something different, we have a powerful motivation to ignore that suspicion.

"Nah," we say to ourselves, "that was nothing," like the child in the dark trying to convince herself that there are no monsters under the bed, working hard to ignore every sound or write it off as branches in the wind or the house settling.

Or how about this: have you ever awakened in the night with a suspicion that you need to pee? I know, it's a crass analogy, but bear with me for a second. Maybe you wake up in the darkest hours of the night, not with a burning need to relieve yourself but just a little, nagging suspicion that if you don't get out of bed and make your way through the dark to the bathroom you're probably not going to be able to go back to sleep.

But of course that's going to be a lot of trouble. The bed is warm and the night is cold. Your room is full of hidden obstacles to bonk your shins and stub your toes. Maybe you have a dog waiting at the foot of the bed for some sign that you're awake so she can greet you with joyful slobber.[7] So maybe, lying there, you tell yourself that you don't *really* need to pee. Maybe you misread the signs. Maybe it was all in your imagination.

You see what I'm saying: when we're comfortable where we are, we're not anxious to find out that we need to move.

---

[7] Mine is named Selah. I don't think she sleeps. She just waits in the dark and takes any sign of movement as a certain sign that day has dawned.

When we're comfortable with the way we've been going, we're not anxious to find out that we need to change directions.

Ironically, we will often remain in situations we aren't even happy about simply because we're more comfortable staying than going. Comfort doesn't necessarily mean happy. Many people are comfortably unhappy. We often find ourselves in situations that we don't really enjoy – we're just reluctant to pay the price that might be required to change things, so we don't. We do our best to ignore the little signs that tell us we have a choice to make, and the clearer those signs get, the more uncomfortable we become.

When God moves, kingdoms collide and when kingdoms collide, we have to choose sides.

That is why "all Jerusalem" was disturbed at the Magi's announcement. It wasn't that they preferred Herod to God's coming King. It was just that they knew that when God moves, kingdoms collide and when kingdoms collide, we have to choose sides.

Of course, if God was really moving then they would pay whatever price was required to be on His side. But was God *really* moving? Did they really *have* to make a choice?

Maybe the Magi were wrong. After all, why should pagan astrologers have any insight into what the God of Israel was doing? Maybe the signs weren't really signs at all…that weird light in the sky probably had a perfectly natural explanation.

But inside, on some level, they must have suspected the truth. And as the years went by, reports began to arrive in Jerusalem of an upstart teacher from Nazareth who could give sight to the blind, still storms and raise the dead. As those reports made their way into Jerusalem, it got harder and harder to ignore the nagging suspicion that God might be moving.

But if God was really moving, then a choice was coming and it was a choice that was going to cost them. So maybe, they told themselves, things weren't really what they looked like; maybe it was all much ado about nothing.

Unfortunately, it didn't really *feel* like nothing…and so they were all shaken up inside.

Choosing Sides

Like the people of Jerusalem, we often miss God's moving because we don't want to have to choose sides. For this reason, we write off the signs and explain away the evidence and keep on hoping that nagging suspicion will go away. It's not necessarily that we prefer our kingdoms to God's…it's just that we'd rather not have to choose between them at all. And so we miss God's moving because we're not motivated to look for it.

The unpleasant reality here is that God is not terribly concerned with our comfort. Our kingdoms may be comfortable, but that matters very little to Him.

Don't misunderstand: God is very much concerned with our *good*, but we often confuse what is comfortable for us with what is good for us. The reality is that they're not the same at all. If you think about it, the history of God's redemption is filled with stories of people whose recognition that God was moving forced them into a very uncomfortable position.

When God moved, Abraham had to choose between his clan and a long journey to a strange land where he had no status, influence or possessions. When God moved, Moses had to choose between remaining with his family and going back to a place full of people who had already tried to kill him. When God moved, Rahab had to choose between obeying the command of her king or protecting the servants of a God her people knew almost nothing about. When God moved, Jonathan had to choose between supporting his own father, Saul, and God's newly anointed king, David. We could go on and on.

...we are sometimes tempted to focus on these wonderful things God has done without giving any attention to what was required of those in whose lives God moved.

The Bible is filled with stories of God moving, and we are sometimes tempted to focus on these wonderful things God has done without giving any

55

attention to what was required of those in whose lives God moved. But I suspect, on some level, we all know that when God moves we must choose, and this sometimes blinds us to the very thing we say we long to see.

Several years ago I was asked to join the staff of a small church. In nearly every way, the situation looked ideal. I had just left my first ministry position as youth pastor of a church that was fairly old, both in terms of its history and its population. Though we had seen God do great things there, my bride and I were always frustrated at how hard it was to overcome the obstacles of tradition and the "this is how we've always done it" mentality.

But this new church was just that: new. It was only about a year old and full of young – well, young*er* anyway – families. Theologically, it was a much better fit too and, best of all, they were passionate about both reaching out to non-believers and equipping Christians to know the truth and live it out consistently.

I was hired as the youth pastor and also asked to fill in "for a while" as the worship pastor. It was a big job, especially considering that I had just started attending seminary full time, but it was exciting and we were up for the challenge. The senior pastor and I quickly became good friends and our first year there flew by. At the end of that year I can remember Coletta and I asking each other why we hadn't left our previous church earlier.

In retrospect, though, there were some unsettling signs even during that first year.

Though the church was only a year or so old when we joined, it had apparently already gone through a church split which had significantly decreased its membership. Throughout that year we heard various comments like, "I sure wish you could have met Doug and Donna," or "I wish the Brown family had stuck around...you would have loved working with them."

When I asked the senior pastor about what had happened, he told me that a retired pastor who had begun attending the church had gathered a following and then begun to challenge the senior pastor on nearly everything. Eventually this retired pastor had left the church and taken a substantial number of families with him. "It really took the wind out of our sails," my friend told me. Though I had never met him I developed a pretty strong dislike for this man who had done this to my friend and my new church.

Since I was still new to the church and getting to know everyone, it took me a while to realize that the loss of members was still going on. Every few months another family left. It was as I was coming to recognize this that I found out that the retired pastor who had caused all the problems hadn't taken his faction with him to start a new church. In fact, they hadn't all stayed together at all but had chosen a number of different places to call their individual church homes. This church-splitting pastor hadn't tried to start another congregation but was attending an already-established church from another denomination. As far as I could tell, he wasn't even seeking any kind of a leadership position, but seemed content to just be part of the body.

Eventually I was asked to go with the senior pastor to speak to some families who were thinking of leaving the church. It was during those interviews that I became aware that the issues were more significant than I had suspected and they had little or nothing to do with the man my friend was blaming so much on. Most of them had to do with leadership decisions made by the senior pastor. There were a few other issues as well, but most of them boiled down to the fact that there was a significant mistrust of my friend the senior pastor.

As the reasons for this came to light I couldn't help but feel that there was some merit to their concerns, but to my shock, the senior pastor's response to these families was pretty much, "Well, goodbye and good luck finding another church."

Even now, more than 15 years later, I can still remember the emotional turmoil of that period in my life. You see, I genuinely thought of the senior pastor as a good friend, and the growing realization that he might be responsible for much of what was happening to the church was very difficult to accept. In retrospect, it's hard to understand how it could have taken me so long to see the truth. On the other hand, I think I know exactly why it was so hard to see: because I knew that if all the signs were real, then I was going to have to make a very hard choice, a choice between my friend and my God.

Obviously, put in those terms, there's no contest. I would never consciously choose loyalty to a man, any man, over loyalty to God. But because the thought of having to make that choice was so difficult, I took a ridiculously long time to see what God was doing. It's amazing how easily, when fear is our motivator, we can convince ourselves that we haven't seen what we thought we saw, haven't heard what we thought we heard.

God very graciously gave me more indications of what was really happening in our church and I eventually came to the realization that I needed to ask the senior pastor to step down. I think I can honestly say that this was the most difficult and painful thing that I've ever had to do, but by the time it came to that, I could no longer deny that this was what God required of me.

I had tried to quietly resign, but while I was actually writing the letter, our denomination's regional superintendent, whom I didn't really even know, called and asked me not to abandon the church.

I had tried to put off doing anything at all, but one of the great saints of our day, a man named Vernon Grounds, caught me in a hallway at Denver Seminary and told me that he knew that I knew what God wanted me to do...and that I needed to do it. I have no idea where he got his information. Well...that's not quite true. I know exactly Who told him; I just don't know *how* He told him. I'll tell you this, though: it was a profoundly unsettling conversation. To say that I came home that day "all shook up" would be an understatement.

I was slow, but I did eventually see that God was moving and there was no point in pretending otherwise. In many ways, that was a great relief. I and another leader in the church very humbly told the senior pastor that we believed he needed to step out of leadership for a while. His reaction was not good, but seeing the way he reacted confirmed for us that he needed to be out of pastoral ministry for a time of soul-searching, healing and reflection.

I won't sugar-coat it: the whole thing was horrible. It remains to this day one of the worst experiences of my life. But what choice did I have? God had moved, kingdoms had collided and I had to choose.

God, of course, is good, and He brought healing and growth to our church in ways I could never have imagined. I remained the youth pastor, which is all I had ever wanted. And that retired pastor who had been blamed for all the turmoil in our church? He became our interim pastor while we searched for a new senior pastor.

He was a godly, humble man from whom I came to learn a great deal. He was such a godly man, in fact, that I often found myself wondering how I could have ever been so blind to how twisted the picture was of him that had been painted for me.

But at the end of the day, I know exactly why it took me so long to see the truth: because seeing the truth about him would have meant seeing the truth of how God was moving and I hadn't been ready to see that yet. When God moves, kingdoms collide and when kingdoms collide, we have to choose sides. Of course I was always going to choose God's side. But for a long time it was easier to pretend that He wasn't moving and that no choice was really required.

I understand exactly how the people of Jerusalem felt when they began to suspect that God was moving. The Magi saw God moving and got on board, but the people of Jerusalem missed it. They missed God moving, not because they preferred Herod to God, not because they didn't want God to move, but because they didn't want to have to choose sides.

Costly Choices

It would be very nice if saying yes to God didn't require saying no to anything else, but we rarely have that luxury.

Far more often than not, saying yes to God requires that we disentangle ourselves from commitments, loyalties and preferences that are not God. They may not be evil in the way that Herod was; they may even be good and worthwhile things. But they are not God and so what they demand cannot be given, not when God is moving. Saying yes to God inevitably requires saying no to someone or something else.

But saying no is hard. Saying no is costly. And because we know this, we are never in a hurry to have to make such choices. And because we would rather not have to make such choices, we often find that we have missed God moving simply because we didn't really want to see it.

How about you? Have you read this chapter with a lingering sense of unease because you have seen signs, heard whispers and suspected that God is moving in your life?

Have you tried to convince yourself otherwise, not because you would ever say no to God, but simply because you know what saying yes might cost you? Are you perhaps missing God moving in your life right now because you know what the people of Jerusalem knew? That when God moves, kingdoms collide and when kingdoms collide we have to choose sides?

If so, know this: God is the only King who wants what is best for you. No other kingdom that demands your time, no other king that clamors for your loyalty, does so because they love you as He does.

Don't get me wrong: I'm not saying that everything God does is about you. It's not. The universe doesn't revolve around you, it revolves around Him. He is the King and the Kingdom exists for His glory, not our good. But His glory and our good are not mutually exclusive. He is the only King for whom this is true.

When God moves and we respond, we are saying yes to a King whose pursuit of His glory will bring us good we can scarcely imagine. That's just the way it is. We are like lamps that can only shine when we are plugged in. But the Source of our power is not static. He moves and we must move with Him.

May you never miss God moving because you were blinded by a choice between kingdoms that you did not want to have to make.

Questions for Discussion

1. *How have you pictured the Magi when you've heard about them in the past? How does your picture of them compare with the reality of whom and what they must have been?*

2. *Can you think of other times in the Bible that unlikely people provided a good model of how we should respond to God?*

3. *Has there been a time in your past where God's moving brought kingdoms into conflict? How did that happen and how did you respond?*

4. Because God's moving often brings kingdoms into conflict, forcing us to choose, responding to God is often costly. However, it is more costly not to respond. What is at stake when we fail to recognize and respond to God moving?

5. Are you currently experiencing anything which may indicate that God is moving? Has this brought kingdoms into conflict? How are you going to respond?

Chapter 3

Dealing with Doubt

Let's just be honest, shall we? Everyone has doubts. Doubt is inescapable. It's the product of being finite creatures in a world that is largely out of our control. We don't know what the weather will be like next month. We don't know if we will be healthy a week from now. We don't know what's happening on the other side of the world right now...or even in our neighbor's house next door.

When we get right down to it, there is very little that we can know with absolute certainty. And that is why we have doubts.

> ...when our doubts become our primary focus, they have a way of obscuring everything else, even huge things like the Almighty moving in our midst.

Doubts may be a natural part of our intellectual landscape, but that doesn't mean they have to dominate our field of view. In fact, we must learn how to keep them from doing so, because when our doubts become our primary focus, they have a way of obscuring everything else, even huge things like the Almighty moving in our midst.

Some philosophers, like Descartes, have even argued that the only thing we can know for certain is that doubt itself exists! That might be a bit extreme, but you get the point: doubt is a permanent fixture of our world, at least on this side of eternity.

Some doubts are relatively insignificant. I don't need to buy milk today because I have plenty at home...or do I? Other doubts are quite serious. When we doubt the existence of God or the reality of His love for us, for instance, we may find ourselves lost, adrift in an existential uncertainty that will significantly affect every aspect of our lives.

This may be one of the reasons why we are often so hesitant to admit to doubts about serious stuff. Somehow, it seems that to acknowledge the existence of such uncertainty would be to give these doubts substance and power. But the simple truth is that nearly everyone has such doubts from time to time. If we can't even know for sure what the weather will be like tomorrow, how can we be certain about spiritual things that take place beyond the reach of our normal perceptions? When we can't remember if we turned off the iron this morning, how can we be sure that we have accurately remembered a spiritual experience from several years ago?

Reluctant Doubters

We all have many doubts. Some are insignificant and some are serious. Some concern mundane, everyday things and others center on transcendent issues like the existence of God or the reality of our spiritual conditions. But all of our doubts spring from the same source: we doubt because we do not know everything.

But if doubt is such an inescapable part of the lives of we fallen and finite creatures, then why are we so reluctant to admit to them? And make no mistake about it, we are reluctant.

Sometimes when I am speaking and sense that the audience is relatively comfortable with me and with one another, I will ask them to raise their hands if they have ever, in the past twenty years, had doubts about God. The hands usually go up slowly, accompanied by furtive glances to the left and right to see who might be watching, but nearly every hand eventually rises. Then I ask them to keep their hands up if they've had such doubts in the last year. Most of the hands stay up. In the last week? Some go down but a majority will usually remain in the air. Then I jokingly ask, "How about today?" and everyone has a good laugh and the exercise is over, but you can see the relief on many people's faces for not having to admit that they have wrestled with such doubts in very recent hours.

I think it is unfortunate that we have to approach the subject of doubt so circumspectly. We all have doubts and we could all benefit from knowing that we are not alone in our uncertainty. But within the Christian world, at least, doubt is often the elephant in the room. Worse than that, we too often treat doubt as though it were the opposite, or even the *enemy*, of faith. How many of us have been told that we need to "have more faith" or "just believe"? These are admonitions that suggest doubt is a danger that will lure us into unbelief.

When I was a young high school student, my family was attending a Baptist church in a small town near to where we lived. One day my Sunday School teacher decided to teach on the subject of evolution. I remember the day vividly, both because of how interested I was in the subject and because of how badly it went.

It was partly my fault, I admit. See, I was a bit of a science nerd (remember plan #2 for my life?) and I wasn't exactly the most tactful teenager that ever lived. So when my Sunday School teacher started talking about the Second Law of Thermodynamics and got it...well, *wrong*, I was quick to point this out. I don't remember exactly what I

70

said, but I'm sure my correction wasn't steeped in gentleness or respect, and that's entirely my fault.

The ironic thing is, I didn't necessarily disagree with the teacher on the subject of evolution itself. I wasn't trying to argue for evolution, I was just saying that his presentation of the Second Law of Thermodynamics was wrong and it didn't conclusively prove evolution wrong.

Unfortunately, that's not how my teacher took it. He saw my correction as an attack on the Creationist position he was teaching. I'm sure there was some simple defensiveness tied up in that, fostered by my own know-it-all attitude, but the fact remains that he didn't admit to a misstatement of the principle or acknowledge that it wasn't the death-knell for evolutionary theory. Instead, he said this: "Listen, Craig, if you're doubting this stuff, then maybe it's because you don't have a saving faith!" At least, that's how I remember it. I might have a couple of the words wrong, but the essence of what he said was clear: my doubts were dangerous signs of unbelief. Worse, my doubts were indications that I didn't have faith, because, presumably, doubt and faith are opposites of one another.

I left that Sunday School class that day and never went back. But I didn't leave the faith. My parents insisted that I had to continue to go to church somewhere, but they were gracious enough to let me pick the place. I wish I could say I began an intense search for a church that was biblically sound and yet could engage in authentic dialogue with a teenager who was trying earnestly to figure out this whole faith thing…but that would be a lie. The truth is I started going to my girlfriend's church. And I don't really know if they were better at dealing with doubts there or not, because I didn't express any of them.

I had learned my lesson. Doubts – and the doubters who have them – are not welcome in church.

Of course that's an overstatement. There are churches that are much more accepting of both doubters and their doubts. But I think they are the exception. As a general rule, Christians are scared of doubt largely because, like my Sunday School teacher, they think that faith and doubt are mutually exclusive.

But they're not. Doubt is not the opposite of faith. The opposite of faith is settled unbelief. Doubt sits somewhere in between belief and unbelief. It is the no-man's land in which all of us sojourn from time to time.

We may not be able to achieve absolute certainty in this life, but that doesn't mean we have to live in constant confusion. We cannot escape doubt, but this does not mean that we must wallow in it.

Doubting Our Way to Faith

To be sure, doubt can play a role in moving us towards unbelief, but it can do the opposite as well. Poor Thomas admitted his doubts and received, alone among the apostles, the opportunity to touch ragged palms and pierced side. His doubts were assuaged with evidence, but evidence that might never have been offered if his doubts had not been confessed. In this way, his doubts moved him deeper into belief, not further from it.

Doubt *can* move us further into faith, but we would be naive to think that it always works this way. I have known atheists whose doubts have toppled their unbelief and I have known those who once claimed to believe change their story too.

Why does doubt sometimes open our eyes to the reality of God moving and sometimes blind us to that very same thing?

So what is the difference? If doubt is inescapable, how can we deal with it in such a way that it broadens and deepens our faith rather than weakening it? Why does doubt sometimes open our eyes to the reality of God moving and sometimes blind us to that very same thing?

Refusing to admit our doubts will not deepen faith. At best, it will paralyze us where we are, perhaps unwilling to backtrack on the path of faith, but also unable to travel further up and further in. However, just admitting that we have doubts, while an important first step, will not necessarily deepen our faith, either. So how can doubt deepen, rather than destroy, our faith?

The answer, I would like to suggest, lies in how we choose to deal with our doubts.

But Now I See

The clearest illustration of the way God calls us to respond to doubt is found in the ninth chapter of the Gospel of John.[8] It is the story of a man, blind from birth, who received his sight when Jesus healed him.

Interestingly enough, as John tells it, the story actually seems to be less about the healing itself than it is about the doubts of those on the sidelines.

> *As he went along, he saw a man blind from birth. His disciples asked him, "Rabbi, who sinned, this man or his parents, that he was born blind?"*

> (John 9:1-2)

The disciples' question may seem strange to us, but it probably reflects a debate among early Jewish rabbis. Much like us, they understood sin to be the ultimate cause of all misery in the world, but they tended to see a more direct correlation between specific sins and specific punishments. Some rabbis thought that birth defects were the result of a generational curse placed upon the parents because of their sin, something they thought was specified in the Old Testament:

> *And he passed in front of Moses, proclaiming, "The LORD, the LORD, the*

---

[8] To give credit where credit is due, I would like to say that some of the way I have come to see what God is saying through this story is thanks to a message by Andy Stanley of Northpoint Community Church.

compassionate and gracious God, slow to anger, abounding in love and faithfulness, maintaining love to thousands and forgiving wickedness, rebellion and sin. Yet he does not leave the guilty unpunished; he punishes the children and their children for the sin of the parents to the third generation. "

(Exodus 34:6-7)

Other rabbis, however, thought that punishment was restricted only to the person who had actually sinned.[9] This presented a problem in the case of someone born with a disability, however, for obvious reasons. The solution, apparently, was that some rabbis developed a complex hypothesis that God created each human soul sometime before it was implanted into a body. During the period between creation and implantation, human souls were capable of committing sins and, as the theory went, particularly grievous sins committed by these souls resulted in their being given bodies with birth defects.

This appears to be the theological debate behind the disciples' question. They wanted Jesus to give them the definitive answer on why this man had been born blind:

---

[9] R. Ammi (a first century Jewish rabbi) said: There is no death without sin, and there is no suffering without iniquity. There is no death without sin, for it is written, The soul that sinneth, it shall die: the son shall not bear the iniquity of the father, neither shall the father bear the iniquity of the son, the righteousness of the righteous shall be upon him, and the wickedness of the wicked shall be upon him, etc.; Shab. 55a:26-27.

was it the result of his parents' sin or his own, pre-incarnate, sin?

Jesus' answer didn't really help all that much:

> *"Neither this man nor his parents sinned," said Jesus, "but this happened so that the works of God might be displayed in him. As long as it is day, we must do the works of him who sent me. Night is coming, when no one can work. While I am in the world, I am the light of the world."*

(John 9:3-5)

Jesus chose to answer their question with a third option, that the man's disability was the will of God so that God could use it to display His power.

It's important not to get sidetracked here by misunderstanding. When Jesus said that "neither this man nor his parents sinned," he wasn't saying that they were all sinless, only that the man's blindness was not directly caused by particular sins they had committed. Rather, he said God allowed this man to be born blind so that he could do something wonderful through it. Of course, no one would ever be born blind if Adam and Eve hadn't sinned, subjecting the world to disarray, disease and decay, so in some sense we can understand that this man's disability *is* the indirect result of sin. But Jesus' point here is that the man's disability is not the direct result of a particular sin but rather of God's will.

I don't know about you, but that's hard for me to accept. In essence, Jesus was saying that God *wanted* this man to be born blind, grow up blind and struggle to survive as a blind beggar, all so that God could break into his life at this moment and do something amazing. How can that possibly be?

I wish I had an easy answer to that question, but I don't. I don't really know how to think about this in a way that will make it all feel better. But here's what I do know and here's what I try to focus on when I find myself butting up against God's inscrutability: I know that God is good and I know that I don't always have the ability to perceive true good.

God's goodness has been demonstrated time and time again. The Cross is the most obvious demonstration of His goodness, but it is by no means the only such demonstration. Likewise, it is undeniable that I cannot always perceive what is truly good. In many ways I'm like a child being given an immunization: I can understand intellectually that what's happening might be "good" but what I feel at the moment is just the pain and that pain obscures any distant horizon where the good may be more discernible.

Because I know that God is good and because I know that I don't have the best track record recognizing true good when I see it, I choose to see Jesus' teaching here through the eyes of faith. This poor blind beggar's life to that point certainly had not been easy, but perhaps what God wanted to do at this moment was a good so great that it would re-cast his every past suffering.

It is also important to understand that saying "God *willed* it" is not necessarily the same thing as saying "God *caused* it." The difference is subtle to discern, but profound in its implications.

This man would never have been born blind if human sin had not so drastically altered the world in which we live. His blindness was therefore a result of sin. What Jesus said here does not mean that God took a perfectly healthy child and broke him so that he would be born blind. The man's blindness could have simply been the result of living in a fallen, broken world, but God had chosen so far not to intervene and fix this particular expression of brokenness so that He could do so at a later time with a greater result. In effect, God withheld what was, from His better vantage point, a small good so that He could do a greater one.

But the way Jesus went about this great and transformative good was certainly strange:

> *After saying this, he spit on the ground, made some mud with the saliva, and put it on the man's eyes. "Go," he told him, "wash in the Pool of Siloam" (this word means "Sent").*

> (John 9:6-7a)

The Gospels record times that Jesus healed people without even being in their presence, so we know that he didn't need to touch this man to heal him. Perhaps more importantly, this is the only miracle reported to us that involved Jesus using a physical medium of any sort. So what's the deal with the mud?

The mud is likely an example of Jesus deliberately upsetting the status quo. A bit later in this passage, John will tell us that Jesus healed this blind man on the Sabbath and that context is extremely important for understanding what Jesus was doing with the mud. You see, the most pious group of religious leaders in those days, the Pharisees, had very strict rules for what you could and couldn't do on the Sabbath. But, contrary to popular opinion today, the Pharisees weren't all heartless zealots completely bereft of compassion. They were well aware of the fact that accidents happen and people get hurt, even on the Sabbath, so they were not opposed to making sure injured people got basic medical care for their wounds, even on the Sabbath.

Now, in those days, basic medical care, especially for cuts and scrapes but really for all sorts of medical conditions, often involved anointing the wound with some kind of oil. In the case of cuts and scrapes, this oil acted to protect the wound from infection.[10] In other types of ailments, the oil may have had a soothing or even anesthetic effect.

---

[10] I'm not saying that 1st century Israelites understood about bacteria and antibiotics, of course. But you don't have to know why something works to know that it works.

Different kinds of oils were used for different conditions. Olive oil was the most readily available to the average person and therefore the most commonly used. But others, like expensive rose oil, were used in some situations or by some people. The Pharisees had determined that treating wounds or medical conditions was acceptable on the Sabbath, but only so long as it made use of materials normally employed for such purposes during the week. Therefore, the average person could use olive oil but not rose oil since rose oil was not normally available to them. Rich people, however, who could normally afford rose oil for themselves, were allowed to use it on the Sabbath since it was a normal material for them.[11]

So what does all this have to do with Jesus and the blind man? Well, very simply, Jesus was deliberately choosing to anoint this man with something that could never have been mistaken for being "acceptable" according to the Pharisees. Not only was he healing on the Sabbath (which the Pharisees would likely have balked at anyway), but he chose to do so in a way that intentionally broke their "rules" for the Sabbath. He was looking to cause controversy, which is exactly what he got.

> *So the man went and washed, and came home seeing. His neighbors and those who*

---

[11] Shab. 14:4 (a collection of early rabbinic teachings on the Sabbath law): If his loins pain him he may not rub thereon wine or vinegar, yet he may anoint them with oil but not with rose-oil. Kings' children may anoint their wounds with rose-oil since it is their custom so to do on ordinary days.

had formerly seen him begging asked, "Isn't this the same man who used to sit and beg?"

Some claimed that he was. Others said, "No, he only looks like him."

But he himself insisted, "I am the man."

"How then were your eyes opened?" they asked.

He replied, "The man they call Jesus made some mud and put it on my eyes. He told me to go to Siloam and wash. So I went and washed, and then I could see."

"Where is this man?" they asked him.

"I don't know," he said.

(John 9:7b-12)

It's probably not possible for us to fully understand the emotion that hides behind this description of what happened. Remember, this was a man who had been blind since birth. He had never seen anything, yet now, after one (albeit strange) encounter with Jesus, he could see. What must it have been like for this man to suddenly perceive the world around him in a way that he had always dreamed of?

In recent years, there have been medical advances that have allowed doctors to restore sight to people born with certain conditions. What's interesting, though, is how hard it is for these people to adjust to and make use of their restored sight. It takes months for their brains to learn what to do with this new information and they never seem to be able to "see" in the way that the rest of us can.[12] But this man that Jesus healed didn't seem to have any of those problems, which suggests that Jesus didn't just heal his eyes but his brain as well, making this an even more profound miracle than it already appeared to be.

One can imagine that this man would have wanted nothing more than a party at this point. He wanted to celebrate! He had been blind but now he could see! As Andy Stanley puts it, he must have been saying, "Somebody get me a cake!"

Rather than celebrating with him, however, the people he met after his healing had a hard time knowing how to respond. Some doubted that he was who he claimed to be, and when he assured them that he was, they wanted to know *how* he had been healed.

The man recounted the highlights of what had happened, and in response to that, the crowd wanted to know *where* this Jesus was. There's probably more to their question than just, "Where is he now"? The fact that this healing occurred on the Sabbath and involved an obvious breaking of the Pharisee's Sabbath rules would have made the crowd

---

[12] For a technical example of this discussion, see: Fine, I., Wade, A.R., Brewer, A.A., May, M.G., Goodman, D.F., Boynton, G.M., Wandell, B.A., and Macleod, D.A. "Long-term deprivation affects visual perception and cortex." *Nature Neuroscience*. September 2003; 6(9): 915-916.

unsure what to think about this man who could apparently heal the blind.

I think it's interesting that the man's response to their questions was "I don't know." This is interesting for two reasons. First, if you watch carefully as the rest of this story unfolds you'll see that there's an interesting contrast that emerges through the use of the phrases "I don't know" and "I know." This is the first instance of a theme that recurs regularly throughout this story. Watch for it. Second, I can't help but find the man's response amusing. I wonder if he wasn't thinking to himself, "I didn't see where he went because I couldn't see *anything* at the time!"

> ...what he didn't know paled in comparison to what he *did* know.

In any event, we see here the first sign of an important division. On one side we have the man who "saw" God moving. On the other side we have some people who had a harder time seeing it because their doubts were getting in the way. But notice, it's not as though the man had all the answers – it's just that what he didn't know paled in comparison to what he *did* know. The fact that he could see seemed to overshadow everything else.

With their questions unanswered, the crowd decided to turn to the religious authorities:

They brought to the Pharisees the man who had been blind. Now the day on which Jesus had made the mud and opened the man's eyes was a Sabbath. Therefore the Pharisees also asked him how he had received his sight.

"He put mud on my eyes," the man replied, "and I washed, and now I see."

Some of the Pharisees said, "This man is not from God, for he does not keep the Sabbath."

But others asked, "How can a sinner perform such signs?" So they were divided.

(John 9:13-16)

Notice that as soon as they heard about the mud, some of the Pharisees became convinced that Jesus was not from God. How could he be? He had broken the Sabbath!

Of course, Jesus had done no such thing. The only thing Jesus had broken was the Pharisees' rules. To be fair, these rules had been developed with a righteous intent: they were put into place to help people know exactly what it looked like to obey God's commandment to honor the Sabbath and keep it holy (Exo 20:8). The intent might have been righteous, but ultimately these were man-made rules. The problem was that some of the Pharisees had made the mistake of confusing their rules with God's.

But not all the Pharisees felt this way, and they rightly wondered how Jesus could have performed this miracle if He were not from God.

Divided, the Pharisees turned to the man and asked what he thought of Jesus, to which he replied, "He is a prophet." Not a bad answer, but certainly not an answer that shows that the man knew the full truth about Jesus. And that's partly the point here: there was still a lot that this man didn't know about Jesus. Just like the Pharisees, the man had unanswered questions. But unlike the Pharisees, the unanswered questions weren't his major concern.

Still divided, the Pharisees summoned the man's parents:

> *They still did not believe that he had been blind and had received his sight until they sent for the man's parents. "Is this your son?" they asked. "Is this the one you say was born blind? How is it that now he can see?"*
>
> *"We know he is our son," the parents answered, "and we know he was born blind. But how he can see now, or who opened his eyes, we don't know. Ask him. He is of age; he will speak for himself."*
>
> *His parents said this because they were afraid of the Jewish leaders, who already had decided that anyone who acknowledged that Jesus was the Messiah would be put out*

of the synagogue. That was why his parents
said, "He is of age; ask him."

(John 9:18-23)

Did you notice the *"we know/we don't know"* theme here in the parents' response? They knew some things and didn't know other things, just like everyone else involved. The real question was which would matter the most: what they knew or what they didn't? Unfortunately, for these parents, the fear of being kicked out of the synagogue kept them on the fence. They were too afraid of the social and financial repercussions of going against the Pharisees on the question of Jesus, so they waffled and deflected the question back to their poor son:

> *A second time they summoned the man who had been blind. "Give glory to God by telling the truth," they said. "We know this man is a sinner."*
>
> *He replied, "Whether he is a sinner or not, I don't know. One thing I do know. I was blind but now I see!"*
>
> *Then they asked him, "What did he do to you? How did he open your eyes?"*
>
> *He answered, "I have told you already and you did not listen. Why do you want to hear it again? Do you want to become his disciples too?"*

Then they hurled insults at him and said, "You are this fellow's disciple! We are disciples of Moses! We know that God spoke to Moses, but as for this fellow, we don't even know where he comes from."

The man answered, "Now that is remarkable! You don't know where he comes from, yet he opened my eyes. We know that God does not listen to sinners. He listens to the godly person who does his will. Nobody has ever heard of opening the eyes of a man born blind. If this man were not from God, he could do nothing."

To this they replied, "You were steeped in sin at birth; how dare you lecture us!" And they threw him out.

(John 9:24-34)

It would appear that most of the Pharisees had decided by this point that Jesus was not from God. They just wanted the man to agree, but he wasn't quite so sure. Perhaps he wasn't so sure that the Pharisees' rules about the Sabbath were the same thing as God's command about the Sabbath. Maybe he wasn't so sure this Jesus had done anything sinful by healing him on the Sabbath. Chances are good that he didn't know what to think about all that stuff, but he did know one thing for sure: he had been blind, but now he could see!

Unfortunately for him, his irritation at the fact that he was stuck trying to answer unanswerable questions – when he just wanted to be out using his new eyes! – got the better of him. He turned sarcastic, asking the Pharisees if they were so interested in this Jesus because they wanted to become his followers.

Infuriated, the Pharisees again fixated on what they did not know: "We don't even know where he comes from!" they said, not meaning that they didn't know his hometown but that they didn't know if he was from God or not.

Finally overcome with frustration, the man unleashed a sarcastic rant that got him kicked out of their assembly and, almost certainly, the synagogue too. But notice that in the midst of this the man had come to a firm conclusion: *if this Jesus were not from God, he could do nothing.*

...he made a decision to focus on what he did know rather than on what he did not.

He probably still had lots of unanswered questions, but he made a decision to focus on what he did know rather than on what he did not. And that focus allowed him to see his next step with enough clarity to take it.

> *Jesus heard that they had thrown him out, and when he found him, he said, "Do you believe in the Son of Man?" "Who is he, sir?" the man asked. "Tell me so that I may believe in him." Jesus said, "You have now*

seen him; in fact, he is the one speaking with you." Then the man said, "Lord, I believe," and he worshiped him.

(John 9:35-38)

Understanding the Pharisees

It would be easy to think that the primary difference between those who saw God moving here and those who didn't was simply a matter of hardened hearts. After all, in Sunday School classes around the world, the word "Pharisee" has become synonymous with "hypocrite," or "legalist." But the reality is that the Pharisees were, like most groups, a mixed collection. Certainly Jesus had some harsh things to say against them as a group, like when he called them (along with the Sadducees) a "brood of vipers" (Mat 3:7), but what we often forget is that Jesus and his disciples had supporters from among the Pharisees as well.

Nicodemus was one such supporter. He first came to Jesus at night, presumably because he was afraid of the possible repercussions among his fellow Pharisees (John 3), but as time went on, he more and more openly supported Jesus (John 7:50) and even provided burial spices and helped to bury Jesus after the Crucifixion (John 19:39-42).

Another interesting thing to consider is that when the Jewish ruling council met to decide what to do about Peter and the apostles who were preaching Jesus' resurrection, it was a Pharisee who stood up and urged caution, saying, "If it is from God, you will not be able to stop these men; you will only find yourselves fighting against God" (Acts 5:39).

My point is not that the Pharisees were all good guys, but simply that we cannot just assume that the reason they missed what God was doing here was because they didn't want God to move. On the contrary, of all the religious sects operating in Israel in the first century, the Pharisees may have been the most poised to see God move.

There was another major group called the Sadducees, but they were generally wealthy and pretty content with the status quo, so they weren't looking for God to arrive and shake things up. A third group, called the Zealots, had taken matters into their own hands. They believed that if God was going to move it would be because He blessed their attempts to harass and harry the Roman occupation forces by guerilla warfare and acts of violence.[13] A fourth group, called the Essenes, had essentially decided that Israel was too corrupt for God to ever move in their midst again. We don't see them in the Gospels because they had withdrawn from culture.[14]

---

[13] It is likely that Barabbas, the man released so that Jesus could take his place on the cross (Mark 15:7-11) was a Zealot. Mark calls him a *stasiastēs* which is translated as "insurrectionist" (NAU) or "revolutionary" (NLT). Interestingly, one of Jesus' followers was known as Simon the Zealot (Mat 10:4), suggesting that he may have come to Jesus from this group.

[14] The closest we see to an Essene in the Gospels is John the Baptist who had some personal practices that were quite similar to what we know of the Essenes. John may have been influenced by a nearby Essene group.

The Pharisees, however, hoped to prepare Israel for God to move in their midst again by getting serious about obeying what He had already told them to do. That was the initial impulse towards creating all the rules and regulations telling people how to, for instance, honor the Sabbath. They called it "putting a fence around the Torah."[15]

The Oral Law that Jesus deliberately opposed by "anointing" the man with mud on the Sabbath day wasn't originally birthed in legalism or from hardened hearts. Actually, it was birthed in a sincere desire to please God. Yes, it turned into legalism. And legalism, as it always does, turned the joyful beat of God's heart into a plodding, joyless march – but it didn't start out that way.

I say again that the Pharisees, of all the first century Jewish sects, were perhaps most poised to see God move in their midst. Yet somehow they missed it. But if they didn't miss it because they were all hypocritical legalists, then why *did* they miss it?

Remember that even as they examined the man whom Jesus healed, there was a division in their ranks. John tells us that some of the Pharisees asked, "How can a sinner do such miraculous signs?" (John 9:16). Clearly there were Pharisees in that group that were open to the possibility that

---

[15] J. Israelstam (an early Jewish rabbi) explains that, "The Torah is conceived as a garden and its precepts as precious plants. Such a garden is fenced round for the purpose of obviating willful or even unintended damage. Likewise, the precepts of the Torah were to be 'fenced' round with additional inhibitions that should have the effect of preserving the original commandments from trespass"; *Aboth* I, 1 n.7

God was moving in their midst. But ultimately the whole group seems to have decided that He wasn't. Why?

A Matter of Focus

I think the answer, as we've hinted at already, is that those who missed God moving ultimately chose to focus on what they didn't know rather than on what they did. They focused on the inexplicable rather than on the undeniable.

> Those who missed God moving ultimately chose to focus on what they didn't know rather than on what they did.

But notice that the once-blind man did exactly the opposite. He focused on the undeniable rather than on the inexplicable.

The once-blind man didn't have answers to all his questions. He didn't know exactly who Jesus was or why Jesus had healed him with spit-drenched mud rubbed into his eyes. He didn't know a lot of things, but "one thing I do know," he said. "I was blind but now I see!"

That is how we deal with doubt so that it does not cause us to miss God moving. We don't pretend it doesn't exist. We don't act as though we are men and women of unassailable faith. We don't refuse to ask hard questions. We don't pretend we have all the answers. But we do choose to focus on what is undeniable rather than on what is inexplicable.

Let me give you a personal example. As I am writing this, Shepherd Project Ministries, where I am privileged to be able to serve as an executive director, is planning a pastors training conference in Zimbabwe for later this year. At the request of several church networks in Zimbabwe, we are taking a team to train church pastors and leaders in Biblical interpretation, Christian doctrine, ministry development, conflict resolution and several other critical topics.

We are all very excited about this conference and feel strongly that God has led us to this project. Along the way there have been several things that have happened which make His leading very clear. However, last week I received the cost estimates for the conference and found myself nearly overcome with doubt.

You see, the last time anything like this was attempted in Zimbabwe, the nation still had its own currency. When that was the case, the exchange rate between U.S. dollars and the Zimbabwean currency was very favorable, making it possible to get very low rates on hotels, conference facilities, food, transportation, etc. However, when Zimbabwe lost their national currency and began conducting business primarily in U.S. dollars (with some British pounds and South African rands thrown into the mix), things got radically more expensive.

Because none of our contacts in Zimbabwe had tried to plan a conference since the currency shift, they had no idea how much more expensive things were going to be. They had given us early estimates based on their previous experience and then later found that more accurate, current estimates were almost five times what they had been expecting.

When I learned this, I was deeply disturbed. Shepherd Project is not a large ministry and the new estimates were beyond our financial resources. As you can imagine, all kinds of doubt suddenly crept in: had we really seen God leading us to get involved with this project? Why would God allow the estimates to be so far off? How could we afford to continue working towards this conference? Should we postpone it, scale it down or call it off?

But in the midst of this, I remembered something important. A few months previously, at a Word Conference we produced in Denver, a young couple approached my oldest daughter, Rochelle, who was working the checkout register at the resource center. They had heard about the project that day and felt led by God to give $250 to sponsor pastors in Zimbabwe so they could come to this event. Rochelle told me this with tears in her eyes because she was sure this couple was making a big sacrifice to give this money. But the story got better. After the couple left and Rochelle had already started telling people about how God had moved them to donate, they came back. They found Rochelle and said that they had gotten to their car and then both immediately felt that they should double their earlier gift, which they did. I cannot tell you how deeply touched Rochelle was by this experience of seeing God provide.

When I found out how much more this conference was going to cost, I felt doubt. I would be lying if I said otherwise. But remembering this couple that God had moved to give so generously gave me confidence that He was in this.

It wasn't just the money; it was the clear sign that God was moving. This couple had seen it, Rochelle had seen it, and we had all celebrated it. Now, as doubts about our ability to produce this event in Zimbabwe began to creep in, I made a conscious decision: I would focus on what I knew rather than on what I didn't. I didn't know why God had allowed us to make plans based on unintentional but radically inaccurate estimates. I didn't know how God was going to provide. But I knew that He had already done several things that I couldn't ignore. And I decided that I would focus on those undeniables rather than on the inexplicables.

Renewed in my resolve to move forward and trust God but, honestly, still deeply affected by these doubts, my youngest daughter, Lynae, and I drove out to rural Kansas for me to speak at a men's event. While I was there, I had the chance to have breakfast with several men and, during our meal, one of them said to me, "Craig, I feel like there's something burdening you. Is there something heavy on your heart this morning?"

Now, I'm not one to volunteer too much personal information easily, especially around strangers, and my first impulse was simply to say that I was fine, if maybe a little bit tired (I'd been up until after 1:00am with another group the night before, so it was completely true). But as I started to say that, I felt God stir. It was nothing dramatic, just a strange little feeling as though divine attention had suddenly focused on me in a particularly…well, *focused* way, I guess.

I felt like God was watching with keen interest. Now, I honestly didn't think that my concern over this conference was affecting me in a way that anyone would have noticed, but I realized that either I was wrong about that or that God had prompted this man to ask his inconvenient question. Either way, I felt like God had backed me into a corner so I gritted my teeth a little and opened up.

I told them just a little bit about the conference and the reasons we felt led to do it, but admitted that with the new cost estimates I wasn't entirely sure how we were going to fund it. I was very encouraged when they asked if they could pray for us and we left to drive back home feeling better.

Somewhere in eastern Colorado, my phone rang and I answered it to find one of the men who had been at that breakfast. He told me he and his wife were closing on a land sale and were trying to decide how best to tithe the profit. Of course at this point I was starting to get pretty excited but then he absolutely floored me when he said that they would like to give $10,000 to the Zimbabwe project!

That didn't cover all the costs, but it was a dramatic improvement over where we had been just two minutes earlier! Lynae and I praised God for that as we made our way through the barren winter farmlands of eastern Colorado.

Then, as the initial excitement about this provision waned a little, I'm ashamed to say that the doubts came creeping back in. I was doing cost analysis in my head as I drove and realizing that, while this gift was going to be a huge help, we still had a lot of money to raise. That was very intimidating for me because I'm a terrible fundraiser. Once I started thinking about what I might need to do to raise the rest of the money, I got steadily less excited, and new doubts started to surface.

But then I remembered this lesson I had learned from the not-so-blind-anymore man in John 9. Yes, there was still a lot I didn't know, but more importantly, there were several things I did know: God had opened the doors for this conference; God had moved a couple to give sacrificially; God had moved a stranger to give generously. These were all things that had God's fingerprints all over them. They simply wouldn't have happened by chance. God had done them.

Once again, I made a conscious decision to focus on what was undeniable rather than on what was inexplicable. God had moved and we were going to trust that He would keep moving all the way through this thing.

As I write this, I've been home from this Kansas trip for less than a week. In that time I've heard from a missions organization that is donating several thousand dollars. I've also been put into contact with the African director of Compassion International who wants Compassion to become a sponsor of the Zimbabwe conference in order to meet pastors there and start working towards a Child Advocacy program in Zimbabwe.

I don't know if we have all the costs covered yet, but we're getting close. If we need additional funds, I don't know where they'll come from. But I do know from Whom they'll come, and I do know that He has done great, undeniable things already, so I will trust Him to do whatever else needs to be done.

Faith and Logic

I am not a man of unshakable faith. At heart, I'm a logical, rational man who prefers careful planning and wise decision-making to bold leaps of faith into unknown waters. I do not believe the pseudo-Christian teaching that says, "If you just have enough faith, God will do anything you ask!"[16] What I'm saying is that I'm not a man for whom faith comes easily.

But as I grow older, I find that I possess, and am possessed by, a deeper and more profound faith than I would have ever thought possible in my younger years. While faith and

---

[16] This teaching, based in part on a very simplistic reading of Mat 21:21 and James 5:15, misunderstands several important Biblical principles. First, it is not the amount of faith that matters but in Whom that faith is put. Second, the more we trust in God, the more we find that what we want God to do is not nearly as important as what God wants to do…and sometimes the two are incompatible. If God wants to teach us patience, our prayer for a quick end to a trying situation may not be granted. I'm not saying that faith is unimportant. On the contrary, it is critical. But this idea that God will do anything we ask if we only believe it enough is simply false.

reason are often thought to be opposites or, at the very least, uneasy compatriots, I have found them staunch allies.

It is the logical decision to focus on what I know rather than on what I do not that has kept me moving forward when doubt would mire me in place. It is the rational choice to make decisions based on what is undeniable rather than what is inexplicable that moves me on, around the bend, where I consistently find answers to the questions that once threatened to paralyze me.

Sometimes, we miss God moving because we deal with our doubts in an unhealthy way, a way that keeps us from ever rounding the bend. We stay rooted where we are, desperate for a change, but too frightened to move forward.

I am not saying that God requires us to leap into the unknown. I am saying that God, in His mercy and love, is in the habit of giving us undeniable experiences all along the way, but that we too often focus on what He hasn't done or on what we don't understand about what He's doing. That has to change.

If you want to make sure you don't miss God moving in your life, then you need resolve to focus on what you do know He has done rather than on what you don't know He is doing. You need to choose to act on what is undeniable rather than on what is inexplicable.

Then and only then, will we, who have been blind, have any chance of seeing.

Questions for Discussion

1. *In your past experiences with church and other Christians, how has the subject of doubt been addressed?*

2. *Why do you think most Christians and churches are so hesitant to acknowledge or deal with doubt?*

3. *Make a list of "generic" undeniables to focus on when you are dealing with doubt. These are things God has clearly done which are not specific just to your life.*

4. *Make a list of "personal" undeniables to focus on when you are dealing with doubt. These are the things you are confident God has done in your own life.*

5. *What kind of doubts are you struggling with right now?*

6. *What are some concrete steps you can take to keep your focus on your list of undeniables when you're dealing with doubt?*

7. *What are some concrete things you can do to try to find answers to the questions that cause you to doubt?*

Chapter 4

Bitter

I'm a busy man. Probably too busy, when you get right down to it, but what can you do? I have a wife to be loved and children to be parented. There are chapters to be written, events to be planned, meetings to be attended, dinners to be cooked, speaking and teaching obligations to be fulfilled. There are papers to be graded and emails to be answered. There's a Bible on my desk to be read and some prayer that needs praying. Some days there's a dog that needs washing and a driveway that needs shoveling or a lawn that needs mowing.

You get the point. I'm busy. You probably are too. And maybe, like me, you sometimes feel guilty about it. If you're someone who deeply longs to see God moving (as I assume you are if you're reading this book), then maybe it even worries you a little. Maybe you're afraid that you might miss God moving because you're too busy to look or listen.

A Very Thin Silence

Maybe you remember the story from 1 Kings 19 where we read that the prophet Elijah was told to go out of the cave where he'd been hiding and prepare to meet God. What follows is more than enough to make busy people fearful:

> *Then a great and powerful wind tore the mountains apart and shattered the rocks before the LORD, but the LORD was not in the wind. After the wind there was an earthquake, but the LORD was not in the earthquake. After the earthquake came a fire, but the LORD was not in the fire. And after the fire came a gentle whisper. When Elijah heard it, he pulled his cloak over his face and went out and stood at the mouth of the cave.*

> (1 Kings 19:11-13)

Scary passage, am I right? What's this "gentle whisper" business? That's how God Almighty chooses to announce His presence?

Actually, it may be worse than that. The phrase "gentle whisper" is the NIV's best attempt at translating a very strange Hebrew phrase here. The NASB went with "the sound of a gentle blowing." The KJV tried "a still small voice." The reason there are so many variations is simply that it's very difficult to know how best to express this concept. Literally, the Hebrew says something like "a thin silence," but who knows what that means?

I'll tell you what it means: whatever it is, it's pretty easy to miss.

See, I'm pretty sure I wouldn't miss God if He showed up in a wind that shattered rocks. I don't think I would miss God if He was announced by an earthquake or heralded by a consuming fire. But a thin silence? I could easily overlook that, especially when I'm so very, very busy.

Work vs. Worship

So maybe you worry about your busyness. And maybe, if you hang out much in a church like I do, you've had some people add a helpful dose of guilt to the worry. Maybe someone has said something like this to you: "You need to slow down. God doesn't want or need your work, He just wants you. But you're so busy thinking that you're working *for* God that you don't have any time to actually enjoy being *with* Him."

I've been told something like this on more than one occasion and I can tell you, there's not much you can say in response. Couched in these terms, where it's a choice between being in a dynamic, intimate relationship with God or slaving away out of some kind of self-deluded attempt to earn His favor, the choice seems pretty clear.

But is it, really? Is the work we do for God really so disconnected from the relationship we have with Him? I'm not sure that it is.

Don't get me wrong. I'm not saying that working for God and relating to Him are the same thing. I'm just saying that serving God and knowing God may be more interrelated than we sometimes think.

Too Busy to Be

I'm not saying that the work we do for God can't get in the way. It certainly can and there is probably no better example of that than the story of Mary and Martha, a classic tale of two sisters, one of whom saw God moving and one of whom didn't. And what blinded the one? Busyness, right?

It has to be busyness, doesn't it? That was Martha's problem, wasn't it? Certainly that's what the Christian living books all tell us. In fact, there appears to be an entire industry that has built up around calling Martha out for being too busy. I won't mention all the titles here, but go to Amazon.com, search on "Mary and Martha," and see how many titles come up. It's a little overwhelming.

It's also a little sad, because what most of them boil down to is a simple black and white message: Mary saw God move and Martha missed it because she was too busy.

But is it really that black and white?

I don't think it is.

Let's look at this famous story as Luke recounts it for us:

> *As Jesus and his disciples were on their way, he came to a village where a woman named Martha opened her home to him. She had a sister called Mary, who sat at the Lord's feet listening to what he said.*
>
> *But Martha was distracted by all the preparations that had to be made. She came to him and asked, "Lord, don't you care that my sister has left me to do the work by myself? Tell her to help me!"*
>
> *"Martha, Martha," the Lord answered, "you are worried and upset about many things, but only one thing is needed. Mary has chosen what is better, and it will not be taken away from her."*

(Luke 10:38-42)

There are several important things to observe here, some of which may not be immediately obvious, especially to a modern English reader.

1. Martha had a serious obligation to provide for her guests.

Did you notice the phrase "opened her home to him"? In the Greek, "opened her home" is a single word, *hupodechomai.* This is a hospitality word and, as such, it speaks of an important concept with deep Old Testament roots.

In the ancient Near East generally, and among the Hebrews particularly, the practice of hospitality was deeply ingrained. When you opened your home to someone, you took on a profound obligation to care for and protect them. This obligation was so profound, in fact, that when the people of Sodom came to Lot's door seeking to do harm to the angels he had unknowingly opened his home to, Lot was willing to give them his daughters instead (Gen 19). Obviously, that raises as many questions as it answers, but the point is simply this: when you opened your home to someone, you became both their protector and provider so long as they were with you.

This word, *hupodechomai*, speaks to this obligation of hospitality. It's the same word that Luke used in Acts 17:7 when describing a charge being brought against a Christian named Jason because he had supported the Apostle Paul and his companion Silas when he "welcomed them into his house." As far as the anti-Christian mob was concerned, Jason was liable for everything Paul and Silas had supposedly done because Jason had given them hospitality. Obviously, hospitality means more than simply making someone feel welcome. In the world of ancient Israel, hospitality went a *lot* further than that.

In the world of ancient Israel, hospitality went a lot further than making someone feel welcome.

This word occurs again in James 2:25 when James used it to recount the Old Testament story of Rahab who "gave lodging" to the Israelite spies. James says that this act of hospitality on her part led to Rahab being "considered righteous." Clearly, *hupodechomai* means more than straightening up and maybe plugging in an air freshener before your guests arrive. The modern notion of hospitality can hardly be compared to the ancient one. In the world of first century Israel, opening your home to someone was serious business.

So what does this have to do with Martha? Well, quite simply, Luke's use of this term, *hupodechomai*, means that Martha had a serious obligation to serve Jesus and his guests whom she had welcomed into her home. Failure to care for their needs would have been more than just a breach of etiquette; it would have been a cause of divine disapproval.

Maybe you remember the story of Simon the Pharisee. It was while Jesus was at Simon's house that a woman came and anointed Jesus with an alabaster jar of perfume and wet his feet with her tears. When Simon objected, Jesus said this:

Do you see this woman? I came into your house. You did not give me any water for my feet, but she wet my feet with her tears and wiped them with her hair. You did not give me a kiss, but this woman, from the time I entered, has not stopped kissing my feet. You did not put oil on my head, but she has poured perfume on my feet.

(Luke 7:44-46)

Obviously, there's a lot more to this story than just a statement about Simon's lack of hospitality, but there is a hospitality issue here: Simon's lack of hospitality was a source of disapproval. It may also be worth mentioning that it is only Luke that recounts this particular statement by Jesus.

Luke also reminds us that Jesus once said, "Whoever welcomes this little child in my name welcomes me; and whoever welcomes me welcomes the one who sent me" (Luke 9:48). The word translated "welcomes" here is *dechomai*, a term closely related to the one Luke used in the Martha story.

This same related term also occurs in Luke 9:5 where we see that Jesus said to the disciples he was sending out, "If people do not welcome you, shake the dust of your feet when you leave their town..." In fact, some form of this *dechomai* root word occurs 26 times in the Gospel of Luke, more than twice the number of occurrences in all the other Gospels combined![17] When we realize that Luke used some form of this term another 22 times in the book of Acts, it becomes clear that this concept of welcoming/receiving was especially important to him.

It seems to me that careful readers of Luke will realize that he has set things up so that we will naturally approve of Martha's activities, at least in theory.

Let's be clear: it was Martha's house, and once she had welcomed Jesus in, she had an obligation to care for him and his disciples, an obligation that Luke has already told us matters a great deal to Jesus. In light of this, simply dismissing Martha as being "too busy" to focus on what was most important is a drastic oversimplification.   This leads us to the second important observation:

2. Luke doesn't say that Martha was "distracted" by the trivial.

To some extent we've already seen this. Martha was discharging a serious obligation of hospitality to the guests that she had received. To simply say she was "distracted" from what was really important misunderstands the role of the host in first century Israel. But there's even more to it than that.

---

[17] Matthew uses it ten times, Mark eight and John only once.

It's very unfortunate that so many English translations of this passage in Luke say something like, "But Martha was *distracted* by all the preparations." This is unfortunate simply because "distracted" is such a negative word and it is not at all clear that this is what Luke intended. The Greek term here is *perispaomai*, a term that is only used this one time in the New Testament, making its translation somewhat uncertain.

Actually, it's a fairly uncommon word across the board. In the Septuagint (the Greek translation of the Old Testament) this term only occurs four times. The first is in 2 Sa 6:6 where it is used to say that Uzzah reached out toward the Ark of God and "took hold of it." Apart from that, it occurs in Ecc 1:13, 3:10 and 5:19 where it seems to have the general meaning of "occupied with." In none of these instances does the word have the connotation of being too concerned with trivial things, something that is often conveyed by the English "distracted."[18]

In several extra-biblical instances, *perispaomai* seems to have been used to convey the idea of someone being "dragged away" by obligations and this would easily fit the context here in Luke. But notice what a difference it makes to say that Martha was "distracted by"

---

[18] For those readers interested in such things, it should be noted that the *peri* prefix might conceivably be intended to convey the sense of being "overly occupied" (cf. Thayer 4187), but this seems to presume too much on the available evidence. There are no clear biblical uses of this term that have a negative connotation and the same observation appears to hold true for the handful of known extra-biblical uses.

something versus being "dragged away by" something. In the former case, she seems a flighty woman who just can't seem to focus on what matters. In the latter case, she seems *forced* to do something.

And what were these other matters that dragged her away? What many English translations render as something like "preparations that had to be made" is literally "services" or "ministries." The Greek term here is *diakonia*, from which we get the word "deacon," which means a servant or a minister.

Rather than saying Martha was "distracted by preparations," it would be more literal to say that she was "occupied with her services," and it might be better to say that she was "dragged away by her services." If this last translation better captures Luke's thought, then we have a very different picture emerging: this is not a woman who was quick to choose working for Jesus instead of being with Jesus; if anything, she may have been reluctant to do precisely that, but fully understood and accepted the seriousness of her obligation as hostess.

Okay, but this might begin to sound like we're venerating Martha and isn't it true that Jesus rebuked her? She's not the heroine of this story, is she? No, she's not. It absolutely must be acknowledged that Jesus rebuked Martha. The question, however, is what did he rebuke her for?

3. Jesus did not say that Mary's choice was better than Martha's.

Translation is always a complicated affair, and at the end of the day it is very difficult to leave personal opinion out of the process. Martha has been seen as the ADD busybody for so long that it is difficult to read anything about her with fresh eyes. This is true for translators as well as for the people in the pews. I think that is probably why some translations record Jesus' declaration in Luke 10:42 as, "Mary has chosen what is better/best" (NIV, NET). Other versions, however, opting for a somewhat more literal translation, say, "Mary has chosen the good portion."

There is a subtle but significant difference between these two renderings. The first creates a clear comparison between the two women: Martha chose badly and Mary chose well. In this vein, it would appear that Mary succeeded where Martha failed. But this raises problems given what we've seen about the importance of hospitality. Could it have been a good thing for Martha to ignore her obligations to her guests?[19] That seems unlikely.

---

[19] Some might suggest that Jesus was asking her to do exactly that and that by doing so was making an implicit statement about social expectations and what was really important. That's possible, but there doesn't appear to be anything in the text here to strongly support this idea. The closest thing to supporting evidence is Jesus' counter-cultural decision to allow Mary to sit at his feet (see below) but his allowing Mary to do this does not mean that he necessarily expected

The second option ("Mary has chosen the good portion") exonerates Mary, certainly, but it doesn't necessarily criticize Martha – at least not for her choice to attend to her hospitality obligations.

The original language here does not compare Martha's choice to Mary's. It simply says that Mary's choice was correct. But doesn't that automatically mean that Martha's choice was wrong?

Not necessarily.

If we are speaking only of the issue of caring for the guests, it is entirely possible that Mary's choice to stay at Jesus' feet was right and Martha's choice to get up and serve them was also right. All that would be needed is for Martha to have a different set of obligations than Mary. But how could that be? Quite simple, actually, if this was Martha's house and not Mary's. If that were the case, then Martha would have had all the obligations that are associated with being the hostess but these same obligations would not have been weighing on Mary...because it wasn't her house.

Is there any way to know for certain that this was Martha's house and not Mary's too? Probably not, but it is certainly not implausible. Remember, Luke identifies Martha as the one who "welcomed" Jesus. If it had been Martha and Mary's home together then we would have expected Luke to say "Martha and Mary

Martha to do the same, especially if she had hospitality obligations to attend to.

welcomed him." And even if they did live together, the obligation of hospitality may have fallen squarely on Martha's shoulders as the eldest sister. Either way, there is good reason to think that Mary was not required to get up from her place at Jesus' feet and serve the guests, not in the same way that Martha was. So it is entirely possible that both Martha and Mary had chosen well.

Mary vs. Martha

But wait. Am I saying that Jesus was equally happy with both Martha and Mary? Of course not. There can be no doubt that Mary was praised and Martha was rebuked. But again, the question is: what was each sister praised or rebuked for?

Mary is easy. Mary was praised for choosing to remain "at the Lord's feet." This is an interesting and possibly loaded phrase. It is likely that it indicates she was learning from him like a disciple. A nearly identical phrase is used of Paul in Acts 22:4 where it is said that he was trained in the Law "under the feet of Gamaliel."

In this context, Luke is probably saying that Mary was being allowed to learn from Jesus as a disciple, just as Peter, John and the others were. This was, in many ways, an unusual thing for Jewish women to be allowed to do. By taking advantage of this grace, rather than giving in to cultural expectations of a woman's role (which would have been for her to get up and help her sister), Mary chose the right option: that provided by God rather than by cultural expectations. For this, Mary was to be praised.

Martha is a little harder. As we've already seen, Martha would have had a serious obligation to care for the guests she had welcomed into her home. To leave them hungry would have been not just culturally offensive, but uncaring. While Mary may not have had this same obligation to serve the houseguests, Martha most certainly did. Moreover, the fact that Luke tells us Martha was "dragged" away by these services suggests that she might even have preferred to stay at Jesus' feet with her sister, but simply didn't have the luxury of doing so.

And yet, Jesus was clearly less than thrilled with Martha. Why?

I don't think it was because she had been dragged away by her obligations. It seems to have more to do with the fact that she was angry that Mary hadn't gone with her. Remember?

> She came to him and asked, "Lord, don't you care that my sister has left me to do the work by myself? Tell her to help me!"

> (Luke 10:40)

It would appear that Jesus didn't say anything to Martha when she got up to attend to her guests. If he was upset that she was leaving, it seems strange that he didn't say so when it happened. Instead, Jesus only rebuked Martha after she came back and vented her frustration with Mary.

117

What Jesus said to Martha is more a defense of Mary's choice than a condemnation of Martha's. Mary, Jesus said, had chosen the right portion which "will not be taken away from her."

That's an interesting thing to say, isn't it? It "will not be taken away from her"? It really appears that Jesus' primary concern here is that Mary shouldn't lose an opportunity that he had given her.

But who would have wanted to take it away? Oh, right: Martha. Martha wanted to take it away. Martha wanted her sister to get up and help her. In fact, she was so upset that Mary wasn't helping, that she kind of went off on Jesus! Can you imagine saying to Jesus, "Tell her to help me!"

Whew! That's serious stuff. You've got to be pretty worked up to give orders to Jesus!

How did she get to that point?

The Slow Boil

It probably started off with a minor frustration: she had probably been sitting there listening to Jesus, but in the back of her mind she was watching the shadows on the wall and knowing that the afternoon was getting on. If she didn't get started on the meal preparations, she would be late getting supper on the table. But maybe she could listen for just a little longer ...

What was that? Did Peter's stomach just growl? Ugh, it did. He was getting hungry. Probably the rest of these men – not much more than boys, really – were getting hungry too. She really was going to have to get to it.

Okay, no real options here. She was in charge of this house and she had guests to feed. She glanced to her sister, but Mary was seemingly oblivious to the late hour.

Typical.

Well, that's what older sisters are for. Have to be a good model. Martha reluctantly climbed to her feet and excused herself, fully expecting that Mary would join her.

But Mary wasn't moving. Martha glanced back at her, tried to catch her eye, move her along ...

But Mary wasn't looking.

Martha ground her teeth. Mary was probably doing it on purpose. So typical – pretending she hadn't noticed Martha get up. Pretending she was just so caught up in the moment that it never even occurred to her to get up and help.

The slow simmer was turning into a roiling boil.

Who did she think she was? Why did she always pull stuff like this? This wasn't the first time...no, no way. She was always doing this kind of thing. Always. Even when they were little kids, she had been like this. Always leaving Martha holding the bag, always expecting Martha to take up the slack.

And here she was doing it again! And on a day like this, with guests like this! It wasn't fair. It wasn't right! How could she sit there with Jesus himself in the house and leave her sister to do all the work!

Come to think of it...what was up with Jesus? Why was he letting her get away with it? Hadn't he seen how Mary pretended not to notice her sister heading for the kitchen? He was so perceptive – how could he not notice? He must have noticed. So why wasn't he saying anything?

He must not care! What other explanation could there possibly be? Jesus just didn't

*care that Mary was leaving her to do it all,
that Mary always left her to do it all.*

*And with that good head of steam built up,
she blew her stack: "Jesus! What's wrong
with you? Don't you care that she's leaving
me to do all the work? I've had it! Tell her
to get up and help me!"*

Silence. A very long, awkward silence.

*Martha was mortified, of course. What had
she just done? Had she just given Jesus an
order? What had she been thinking? What
had caused her to blow up like that?*

The Poison of Bitterness

You've probably figured it out by now. What went wrong
was a little thing that most of us struggle with to one degree
or another: *bitterness*. Martha's problem wasn't that she
was busy; her problem was that she was bitter about it.

Let's get something straight: work is a good thing. God
invented it, after all. When He first made Adam and Eve,
He told them, "Be fruitful and increase in number, fill the
earth and subdue it" (Gen 1:28). Subduing takes some
doing. It's hard work.

And remember, this was before the Fall. Don't make the
mistake of thinking that hard work was part of the Curse,
because it wasn't. The Curse introduced *futile* work, not
hard work. Hard work was a grace gifted to humans from

> **The goodness of the work we do largely depends on the attitude of the heart performing it.**

the beginning because in hard work there is meaning and significance. Work is good.

However, the goodness of the work we do largely depends on the attitude of the heart performing it. When a new bride works to place a meal in front of her beloved because he is her beloved, her work is good. When a husband eases out of the house in the dark to get to the office early so he can help his daughter pay for college, his work is good. When children clean the house because they know their parents are busy sacrificing for them, their work is good. When a pastor slaves over his sermon because he wants to please God and bless his congregation, his work is good.

But…when the plate is slung angrily in front of a husband who stopped saying thank you years ago…when the door is slammed loudly in the early morning dark, intended to jar awake a family that is never satisfied with what is provided…when the cleaning is half-hearted and sloppy with resentment…when the sermon is laced with subtle recriminations for a congregation that never seems to stop grumbling…the work is not so good.

Bitterness poisons the well of our souls, leaching away our joy and corrupting everything that comes out of us. From a heart toxic with bitterness, words can only wound and work can only reproach.

If Martha hadn't blown her stack, I can guarantee that everyone would have heard the pot being stirred with ever-increasing force, the plates being set down more and more loudly, the dull thuds reverberating with judgment. And the meal, regardless of how tasty, would have been hard to swallow. Bitterness does that to things.

Work is good because it was ordained by God and gives us something to lay at His feet. But work poisoned by bitterness leaves us only with a sludge we would never offer to anyone, let alone the Almighty.

Now, I'm not saying that Martha was a woman constantly consumed by bitterness. On the contrary, I strongly suspect that she was someone who typically served with joy. I imagine on most days she would have welcomed the opportunity to prepare a meal for Jesus and his disciples. If I had to guess, I would say she typically took great pleasure in her ministry of hospitality.

And I doubt that she was really all that upset about having to take care of the details that day either. It was just that it was such a unique opportunity to have Jesus teaching right there in her living room, and having to excuse herself and then watch her sister just keep sitting right there…

From Worship to Whining

See, that's when it always happens. That's when bitterness

Bitterness finds its way in when we forget Who it is, ultimately, that we're serving.

gets its foot in the door: when we lose focus. Bitterness finds its way in when we forget who it is, ultimately, that we're serving…when our eyes stop looking at Jesus and start looking at the others who we think should be doing for Jesus what we're doing for him or, at the very least, who should be appreciating all that we do for him.

At least that's how it happens for me.

A couple of years ago, my family and I were putting together a Christmas set at our church. I tend to think big when it comes to stuff like that and the project had gotten pretty involved. What started out fun had gotten tedious, and I have to admit I wasn't exactly oozing joy.

On the contrary, I was headed down Martha's road to bitterness.

See, at first, I was just wishing we had some more people there to help. Of course, I hadn't actually asked anyone else to help (had Martha?), but you know how it is – probably no one would have come anyway. I mean, the children's ministries at church had been begging for volunteers recently and no one was stepping up to the plate.

They just didn't care about ministry all that much, you know? And if they wouldn't help out with children, why would I expect them to help out with a Christmas set? It's not like they would understand how this was even ministry. It's not like they would see the value in creating a worship space that would engage all the senses and inspire deeper devotion. Our congregation just doesn't think like that…they don't appreciate that sort of thing the way they should; that is, the way *I* do.

Actually, they probably wouldn't even care how much time we'd put into this at all. They would probably say, "Oh, that looks nice," and never give another thought to how much effort it took or what sacrifices had been made to do this for them. So why were we bothering? Why was I always throwing these pearls before…

And then my daughter Rochelle had to go and blow the good head of steam I was getting up.

"You know, this is like a really big birthday present for Jesus!"

"This is going to look so good," she said. "You know, this is like a really big birthday present for Jesus! How cool is it that our family gets to do stuff like this?"

Shoot. Right…a birthday present for Jesus. This was for Jesus, not the congregation. I mean, I wanted God to take what we were doing and bless the congregation too, but ultimately, it had been conceived as an act of service, of worship.

Where had I gone wrong? How had I gone from worship to whining?

Quite simply, I had lost my focus. I had stopped looking at Jesus. And when I stopped looking at Jesus, I found myself noticing all kinds of things – some real, but most imagined – that just irritated me, angered me, embittered me. And that little tendril of bitterness began to poison the well of my soul, leaching away my joy.

So I get it. I understand what happened to Martha. I'm not particularly prone to bitterness, but I'm not immune to it either. If I'm not careful, my most profound acts of serving can become a toxic sludge I wouldn't lay at my worst enemy's feet, let alone at my Lord's.

The 80/20 Rule

Being busy is not necessarily a problem, but being bitter about it is.

Have you heard about the 80/20 Rule? It's a principle that church leaders like to bandy around a lot that says 80% of the work in a church is done by 20% of the people.

It's a stupid rule.

I'll tell you why: 20% of the people cannot do 80% of the work. At most, 20% of the people can do 20% of the work. That just means that 80% of the work isn't getting done.

Now that's something I really believe. The church is not doing in the world what we are here to do. Why not? Well, there are many reasons, but one of them is that 80% of the people who go to church *just* go to church. When the service is over, they don't go back into the world thinking of themselves as Kingdom-workers. Their faith is a compartmentalized, shallow thing rather than an engine for change. They don't do much else, so about 80% of the work God has given His people to do in the world just isn't getting done.

And here's the interesting thing: an awfully lot of the 80% use Martha as an excuse. "Sorry," they say, "but I just don't think I should get involved in this ministry effort. I'm already so busy and, hey, I don't want to be like Martha, do I? Too busy doing stuff for God that I'm not taking time to be *with* Him!"

Of course you shouldn't give up being with God to do things for Him…but why should those two things be mutually exclusive?

Listen, if that's you, stop it. Martha's problem wasn't that she was busy. Martha's problem was that she had started down a road that would have ultimately rendered all her hard work a hollow sham. But I think Jesus was just fine with Martha's work. After all, Jesus never told Martha to sit down, chill out or slow up. He never told her to forget about caring for her guests. He said she was "worried and upset about many things." He didn't say she was "too busy" or "serving when you should be sitting." He said she was anxious and disturbed, which seems most likely to be a response to her irritation and frustration with Mary.

Martha's problem wasn't being busy, so if you're part of the 80%, don't justify your reluctance to get involved by pointing to Martha.

But if you're part of the 20%, then I have another, perhaps harder word for you: don't make Martha's mistake. Don't let bitterness poison the well of your soul.

> **Don't let bitterness poison the well of your soul.**

I don't think I've ever heard the 80/20 Rule cited by anyone but church leaders. And you know what? There's always an undercurrent of bitterness there.

I get it. I know how easily it can happen. Bitterness never begins big. It happens by slow degrees, every one of which depends on our eyes being fixed on something other than the One we ultimately serve.

I understand. People disappoint us. Sometimes they fail us and they just don't appreciate us. There will be times when you will be taken for granted, whether in your church or in your marriage or in your friendships. At work you might not get the promotion you deserved or the recognition you've earned. It happens.

But you cannot let bitterness take root. You cannot let it poison your soul. You cannot.

At stake is not simply the ability to put anything worthwhile at Jesus' feet. At stake is the ability to see Jesus at all.

Blinding Bitterness

If it is allowed to do its toxic damage, bitterness will ultimately blind us to the reality of what God is doing, of how He is moving. Bitterness will keep us from seeing God at all.

Mary saw what God was doing. Jesus was throwing the doors of the Kingdom far wider than anyone in ancient Israel would have ever expected. He touched lepers, welcomed sinners, engaged Gentiles and taught women as equals. Mary saw what was happening.

Martha, however, almost missed it, not because she was too busy working *for* Jesus, but because she was no longer looking *at* Him. She had lost sight of the one thing – of the One – that we cannot afford to lose track of.

Fortunately for Martha, her brush with bitterness was short-lived. It would appear that Jesus' soft words corrected her course and she recovered her joy.

But I don't think she stopped being busy. In fact, every time we see Martha in the Gospels she seems to be busy with some task or another. She doesn't seem to have slowed down, eased up or chilled out. But she does seem to have remembered why and who she was busy serving in the first place.

Without bitterness to poison her soul and blind her, she regained her ability to see God moving in great ways. In fact, one of the most profound statements of revelation in all of the Gospels was given to Martha:

Jesus said to her, "I am the resurrection and the life. He who believes in me will live, even though he dies; and whoever lives and believes in me will never die. Do you believe this?"

"Yes, Lord," she told him, "I believe that you are the Christ, the Son of God, who was to come into the world."

(John 11:25-27)

This exchange between Jesus and Martha is profound in several ways. First, it is one of the most explicit revelations of himself that Jesus gave to anyone. Would Martha have received this great honor if she was a woman too busy to really "get" Jesus? Second, Martha's declaration of faith here is remarkably similar to the one made by Simon Peter following Jesus' transfiguration, recorded in Matthew 16:16: "You are the Christ, the Son of the living God."

Simon Peter, of course, became the leader of the early church following Jesus' ascension, and it would appear that part of the reason for his selection to this role was based on his declaration of faith. But it may also be worth noting that Jesus explicitly said that Simon Peter's declaration was not simply a matter of the young man's excellent discernment. Rather, Jesus said, "Blessed are you, Simon son of Jonah, for this was not revealed to you by man, but by my Father in heaven" (Mat 16:17).

In other words, Simon Peter didn't say what he said about Jesus because he had figured it out on his own, but because he had heard the voice of God speaking this truth to his heart.

Given this, the similarity between Simon Peter's statement of faith and Martha's statement of faith is all the more remarkable. It strongly suggests that Martha's statement, like Simon Peter's, was not a matter of her wisdom but a matter of divine revelation. In other words, God was moving in her as well and she saw exactly what was going on.

So, rather than being a purely cautionary tale, Martha is for us an example of someone who had some trouble seeing God moving at a particular point in her life, but who subsequently recovered her ability to see.

Bitterness does not need to leave permanent scales over our eyes. Those scales can be removed if only we will refocus on the One we should never have lost sight of in the first place.

Bitterness does not need to leave permanent scales over our eyes.

Questions for Discussion

1. *Sometimes busyness can be an obstacle for intimacy with God. Has this ever been a problem for you?*

2. *What do you think of the idea advanced in this chapter that Martha's greatest problem was not busyness but bitterness?*

3. *Has bitterness ever "poisoned the well of your soul"? Are you presently struggling with bitterness? In what ways?*

4. What things are most likely to take your focus off Jesus and allow bitterness an open door into your life?

5. What steps do you need to take to refocus on Jesus and stop giving bitterness an open door in your life?

Chapter 5

Too Happy to See

Bitterness is not the only thing that can make us lose our focus and miss God's moving. Sometimes we lose our focus and miss God's moving because of joy.

Well, perhaps *joy* isn't quite the right word for what I'm talking about here. Maybe *happiness* speaks more directly to what I have in mind. As I see it, *joy* is best understood as an experience of contentment that transcends our circumstances, whereas *happiness* is deeply rooted in our feelings about a particular set of circumstances. This distinction can be overdone and I will be the first to acknowledge that there is considerable overlap between the two terms in common usage. I must also acknowledge that one cannot always read this kind of distinction into the two different terms as we find them in the Bible. The Greek and Hebrew terms for "joy," "happiness" and "rejoicing" are often used interchangeably.

However, it seems to me that we need to be able to distinguish between two different types of gladness – the one circumstantial, the other transcendent – and these two words will serve that purpose in many instances.

Why do we need to be able to distinguish between types of gladness? Simply because there is a gladness which depends on what is happening now and a gladness which depends on what we know *will* happen, but which we may not yet have seen fully realized.

On a very superficial level we experience this distinction daily. I am never happy about getting out of bed, but I can be joyful about rising because I look forward to what the day holds. I am never happy about cleaning my office, but I can be joyful about the process because I look forward to a clean workspace. I am not happy about working out, but I can be joyful about going to the gym because I look forward to being better able to enjoy hikes with my family this summer.

Spiritually speaking, this distinction in terms is even more necessary, simply because we regularly face circumstances in this life which we do not like, but which we must approach in light of what God has promised. We are told, for instance, that *in all things God works for the good of those who love him, who have been called according to his purpose* (Rom 8:28). In other words, God will bring good out of even the worst of our circumstances and we must somehow learn to approach our present circumstances in light of this coming redemption of them. We need not be happy about what is happening, but we must take joy in what God will do with what is happening.

This is not simply an optional approach to difficult circumstances – it is a command. In James 1:2 we are told to *consider it pure joy, my brothers, whenever you face trials of many kinds.* James goes on in this passage to speak of the good things that he knows God brings out of such trials. I do not believe he is calling us here to take pleasure in, or be happy about, the trials themselves, but to rest in a more transcendent joy which depends on the coming redemption of them.

That is why I say that we need to make this distinction between joy and happiness. It is possible, though it is never easy, to have joy even in very difficult circumstances; but happiness, by its very nature, is confined to those circumstances which we find inherently pleasant.

The problem is that, for most of us, the distinction between joy and happiness is a very slippery one, simply because we cannot see beyond the present moment in any meaningful sense. We find it very difficult to be content when things are unpleasant, even when we understand that those circumstances are transient and insignificant, pale shadows to the greater glories God has promised are coming.

The root of the struggle, I think, is not that our present circumstances are larger than coming glories, but only that they are *closer*. Put your hand close in front of your eyes and you will find that it blocks out nearly everything else. Your hand, of course, is quite small compared to the room you're sitting in right now, but if it is brought close enough, it eclipses even the things which are many hundreds of times larger.

Consequently our circumstances exert an unjustifiably great influence on us, robbing us of a lasting joy simply because we are not happy in this one present moment.

But I digress. My point is not that unpleasant circumstances make it hard for us to see God moving, though that is true enough. My point is, rather, that *all* circumstances can cause us to miss God's moving if we allow them to. This is true for unpleasant circumstances, obviously, but it is just as true for pleasant ones. And so I say that sometimes we lose our focus and miss God's moving because of happiness.

Provision

In the sixth chapter of the Gospel of John we find an account of two groups of people who both had the opportunity to see God moving, but one group missed it. Let's see why.

As John 6 begins, we find that Jesus had crossed over to the far shore of the Sea of Galilee and a great crowd had followed him. What was it about Jesus that attracted them? John tells us they were there because "they saw the miraculous signs he had performed on the sick" (John 6:2).

This is a perfectly understandable motivation for them to follow Jesus. After all, he had performed miracles of healing at least in part because those miracles demonstrated who he was. But as we shall soon see, the crowds were less interested in who Jesus was than in what Jesus could do for them.

> ...the crowds were less interested in who Jesus was than in what Jesus could do for them.

Then Jesus went up on a mountainside and sat down with his disciples. The Jewish Passover Feast was near.

When Jesus looked up and saw a great crowd coming toward him, he said to Philip, "Where shall we buy bread for these people to eat?" He asked this only to test him, for he already had in mind what he was going to do.

Philip answered him, "Eight months' wages would not buy enough bread for each one to have a bite!"

Another of his disciples, Andrew, Simon Peter's brother, spoke up, "Here is a boy with five small barley loaves and two small fish, but how far will they go among so many?"

Jesus said, "Have the people sit down."

There was plenty of grass in that place, and the men sat down, about five thousand of them. Jesus then took the loaves, gave thanks, and distributed to those who were seated as much as they wanted. He did the same with the fish. When they had all had enough to eat, he said to his disciples, "Gather the pieces that are left over. Let nothing be wasted." So they gathered them and filled twelve baskets with the pieces of the five barley loaves left over by those who had eaten.

After the people saw the miraculous sign that Jesus did, they began to say, "Surely this is the Prophet who is to come into the world!"

(John 6:3-14)

Interestingly, this passage begins with a test given to Philip. It may not be immediately clear what Jesus was testing exactly, but the fact that John specifically mentions the Passover Feast is an important clue. As you may recall, the Passover was a Jewish celebration that went back to the time of the Exodus, when God set His people free from slavery to Egypt. On the night before they were finally released, the Israelites were required to sacrifice a lamb and put some of its blood on the doorways of their homes. During the night, God "passed over" the homes of the Israelites that had been marked by the blood of this sacrifice, but struck down the firstborn of their Egyptian oppressors.

For obvious reasons, the Passover Feast held great significance for the Jewish people generally, but it held even greater significance for Jesus specifically. As we now know, the first Passover and all the subsequent celebrations of it ultimately pointed to Jesus' sacrifice (on Passover, no less) as the Lamb who takes away our sin. In other words, the Passover was not just a celebration of what God had done, but it was also a foreshadowing of what God would do.

But the Passover not only pointed forward in time…it also pointed *backwards*. No reader of the Old Testament can forget the story of Abraham and Isaac in which God told Abraham to sacrifice his only son, Isaac. In faith, though no doubt with weak and trembling legs, Abraham submitted to God and set out to do exactly that. But once

God saw that Abraham was committed to obedience, He stopped Abraham and provided a substitute.

The sensitive reader will no doubt already see the parallel between this story and the fact that, in the person of Jesus, God provided a substitute sacrifice for us as well. But just to make sure no one could ever miss it, the story of Abraham and Isaac also includes the following conversation between them:

> *Abraham took the wood for the burnt offering and placed it on his son Isaac, and he himself carried the fire and the knife. As the two of them went on together, Isaac spoke up and said to his father Abraham, "Father?"*
>
> *"Yes, my son?" Abraham replied.*
>
> *"The fire and wood are here," Isaac said, "but where is the lamb for the burnt offering?"*
>
> *Abraham answered, "God Himself will provide the lamb for the burnt offering, my son."*

> (Genesis 22:6-8)

God Himself will provide the lamb for the burnt offering.

Remember that these words were written at least twelve centuries before Jesus, and they recount an incident that was already many centuries past even then. Yet even here we see the outline of God's plan of salvation. I doubt very much that Abraham knew how his words of faith would reverberate through history, resonating with God's people throughout time until, with a clarion bell of realization, we would see the Lamb of God, served up for our sake on a wooden stake atop a barren hill. God Himself will provide the lamb, Abraham said. How right he was.

As Jesus looked out on the crowds following him, just a day or two before the Passover, and asked Philip, "Where will we get bread for all these people?" it seems clear that the answer was supposed to be: "God will provide."

Unfortunately, Philip seems to have failed this little test. His response betrayed the limits of his vision. He simply couldn't see beyond the impossibility of their circumstances: "Eight months wages would not buy enough bread for each one to have a bite!"

Andrew's response was a little better: "Here is a boy with five small barley loaves and two small fish...but how far will they go among so many?"

Clearly, like Philip, Andrew struggled to see over the wall of impossibility, but at least he was stretching up on tiptoes, trying to get a glimpse of the elusive horizon of hope. He had found some food at least, though we don't know how exactly. Perhaps the boy had volunteered it or perhaps Andrew had been trying to be proactive, searching for options. In any event, though he had little optimism, he offered Jesus what he had.

It wasn't much, but God really doesn't need much, does He? In fact, He needs nothing. He is the Flinger of the Stars, the God who brought light (which is something) out of the dark (which is nothing). He created all things simply by His word. No, He doesn't need anything at all. But, He often waits for the tiniest mustard seed of faith so that when He moves, His work has something in us that it can attach to.

> **He often waits for the tiniest mustard seed of faith so that when He moves, His work has something in us that it can attach to.**

Like a snowflake that grows into a dazzling work of art around a single speck of dust, our faith is a seed around which God works His wonders.

And apparently this little offering from Andrew and the young boy was enough. Jesus took it and fed the thousands. It was a miracle in every sense of the word. I have heard preachers claim that this was really a social marvel – that this little boy's offering inspired everyone else to pitch in and share with one another – but such an interpretation completely misses John's own assessment of what happened: *After the people saw the <u>miraculous sign</u> that Jesus did...* (John 6:14). The Greek term here is *semeion* and it is used throughout John's Gospel to speak of supernatural acts that cannot be accomplished by any natural means or process.

Ironically, anyone who wants to deny the supernatural character of this miracle will find it impossible to understand what happened next:

> *So Jesus, knowing that they intended to come and make him king by force, withdrew again to the mountain by himself.*

(John 6:15)

If this had simply been a matter of people being inspired by the little boy's generosity, then why would they have wanted to make Jesus king?

No, they wanted to make Jesus king because they had just seen his ability to provide for them. Can you imagine a better king than one who could feed vast crowds with almost nothing? A king who could take the smallest offering and turn it into a feast?

No wonder they wanted to make him king, even if they had to do it by force. But of course if Jesus had wanted to be recognized as king, He could have just stayed at the Father's side. The incarnation, the manger, the childhood in Nazareth – none of these would have been necessary if his goal was to be exalted. No, Jesus was after something else, and so He withdrew from the crowds and their adulation.

Now here's where it gets interesting.

Provider

That evening, Jesus' disciples went down to the lake, got into a boat and "set off across the lake for Capernaum" (John 6:17). I have no idea what they were intending to do. John simply doesn't say. What we do know is that Jesus decided to join them, but since they were already pretty far out on the lake, he had to arrange other transportation:

> *By now it was dark, and Jesus had not yet joined them. A strong wind was blowing and the waters grew rough. When they had rowed three or three and a half miles, they saw Jesus approaching the boat, walking on the water; and they were terrified.*
>
> *But he said to them, "It is I; don't be afraid."*
>
> *Then they were willing to take him into the boat, and immediately the boat reached the shore where they were heading.*
>
> (John 6:17b-21)

By all appearances, this is the same event that is also described in Mat 14, but John's version is much abbreviated. Matthew's account is unique in including the fact that, before getting in the boat, Jesus invited Peter to join him on the water, but other common details make it certain that these are two accounts of the same lake crossing. This is not a contradiction; John was likely counting on his audience already being familiar with that part of the story from Matthew's Gospel and did not feel the need to repeat it here simply because it wasn't needed for the point he was making. But what is that point? Let's continue:

> *The next day the crowd that had stayed on the opposite shore of the lake realized that only one boat had been there, and that Jesus had not entered it with his disciples, but that they had gone away alone.*
>
> *Then some boats from Tiberias landed near the place where the people had eaten the bread after the Lord had given thanks.*
>
> *Once the crowd realized that neither Jesus nor his disciples were there, they got into the boats and went to Capernaum in search of Jesus.*
>
> *When they found him on the other side of the lake, they asked him, "Rabbi, when did you get here?"*

(John 6:22-25)

We don't need to get hung up on the fact that they called Jesus "Rabbi" here.[20] While that title is obviously less exalted than "Lord," there is no reason to think that they

---

[20] Some commentators do find this title to be significant (cf. Leon Morris, *The Gospel According to John* [William B. Eerdmans Publishing Company, 1971], 357), but I find no compelling reason to think "Rabbi" here is anything other than a term of respect.

were being disrespectful. Given what they knew of Jesus at this point, they simply didn't know what else to call him. It is possible that, having seen Jesus' reluctance to become king the night before, they were attempting to placate him by using a title they thought he might respond more positively to. In any event, what's most important here is the fact that they were still pursuing Jesus, yet Jesus' response to them indicates they were doing so for the wrong reasons:

> *Jesus answered, "I tell you the truth, you are looking for me, not because you saw miraculous signs but because you ate the loaves and had your fill. Do not work for food that spoils, but for food that endures to eternal life, which the Son of Man will give you. On him God the Father has placed his seal of approval."*

> (John 6:26-27)

Ironically, Jesus here was chastising them for not paying attention to the miracle itself. I say this is ironic because at another point in his ministry, Jesus chastised another group for what appears to be exactly the opposite: *As the crowds increased, Jesus said, "This is a wicked generation. It asks for a miraculous sign, but none will be given it except the sign of Jonah"* (Luke 11:29). In this latter instance, Jesus faulted the crowd for *wanting* a miraculous sign whereas in the former instance, he faulted them for *ignoring* the miraculous sign. Why the difference?

148

The difference appears to be that the first crowd had been given a sign but were ignoring its main significance whereas the second crowd had already seen the significance of the signs, but still demanded more "proof." As I said earlier, Jesus used miracles to demonstrate who he was, but he also understood that, for some people, no amount of evidence will ever suffice.

In essence, the two crowds were focused on two entirely different things. The second crowd was focused on heaven, but in a demanding way, insisting that heaven deliver more proof before they would change their opinion about what was happening on earth. This crowd, however, seems to have been so fixated on what was happening on earth that they did not see the hand of heaven behind these events.

That's hard to understand. After all, hadn't they just witnessed a miracle, and don't all miracles come from heaven?

Yes, of course they do, but it is possible to get so caught up in what heaven gives us that we forget about heaven itself. It is possible to become so focused on what God has provided that we forget about the One who provided it. And isn't that exactly what Jesus said was happening here? *"I tell you the truth,"* Jesus said, *"you are looking for me not because you saw miraculous signs but because you ate the loaves and had your fill."*

For a crowd of people who were probably used to going about life with grumbling bellies, the *miracle* of the loaves and the fish had been largely eclipsed by the loaves and the fish themselves. But for Jesus, the food was simply a provision, but it was the Provider he really wanted them to see. Otherwise, they would be in danger of missing a gift far greater than bread and fish:

> …the *miracle* of the loaves and the fish had been largely eclipsed by the loaves and the fish themselves.

Then they asked him, "What must we do to do the works God requires?"

Jesus answered, "The work of God is this: to believe in the one he has sent."

So they asked him, "What miraculous sign then will you give that we may see it and believe you? What will you do? Our forefathers ate the manna in the desert; as it is written: 'He gave them bread from heaven to eat.'"

Jesus said to them, "I tell you the truth, it is not Moses who has given you the bread from heaven, but it is my Father who gives you the true bread from heaven. For the bread of God is he who comes down from heaven and gives life to the world."

"Sir," they said, "from now on give us this bread."

It's interesting that the crowd asked for another sign and even specified the kind of sign they wanted – bread from heaven – apparently without seeing that they had already been given this exact sign! This story practically drips with irony.

The Bread of Life

But Jesus remained patient, trying to draw their attention away from the provision and back to the Provider who had something far better than bread to give them:

> *Then Jesus declared, "I am the bread of life. He who comes to me will never go hungry, and he who believes in me will never be thirsty. But as I told you, you have seen me and still you do not believe. All that the Father gives me will come to me, and whoever comes to me I will never drive away. For I have come down from heaven not to do my will but to do the will of him who sent me. And this is the will of him who sent me, that I shall lose none of all that he has given me, but raise them up at the last day. For my Father's will is that everyone who looks to the Son and believes in him shall have eternal life, and I will raise him up at the last day."*

(John 6:35-40)

We see here that Jesus wanted to do so much more than fill their stomachs. He wanted to satisfy longings and hungers that went so much deeper, whether they recognized them or not. He didn't just want to give them bread. He wanted to give them himself; and through him, eternal life lived in fellowship with the Father. The miracle of the fish and the loaves had simply been, as John labeled it, a *sign*. It pointed beyond itself to God, beyond the provision to the Provider.

Unfortunately, the crowd had some trouble focusing:

> *At this the Jews began to grumble about him because he said, "I am the bread that came down from heaven." They said, "Is this not Jesus, the son of Joseph, whose father and mother we know? How can he now say, 'I came down from heaven'?"*
>
> *"Stop grumbling among yourselves," Jesus answered.*

(John 6:41-43)

What follows in John 6 is an extended teaching by Jesus in which he identifies himself as the "bread of life" and even foreshadows the coming Last Supper and His crucifixion. For our purposes here, perhaps the most interesting part of this speech comes in 6:58 when he said, *"Your forefathers ate manna and died, but he who feeds on this bread will live forever."* Again we find the connection between this miracle of Jesus and the flight from Egypt commemorated

152

by the Passover festival. God's provision of manna in the desert was an integral part of the story of Israel's exodus from Egypt. But the manna wasn't supposed to be the main focus. The main focus was supposed to be on the One who had caused the manna to fall.

In the same way, the miracle of the bread and the loaves was just to get their attention. It was supposed to draw their attention beyond the near horizon of their present circumstances. Once again, Jesus was trying to draw the audience's attention away from the provision which was right in front of them to something far greater and, most importantly, to the One who longed to provide it if only they would look to Him.

What Jesus understood fully and what so few in the crowd could see is that full bellies mean nothing when our souls are wasting away. God is the Compassionate One and He cares deeply about all our needs, both physical and spiritual, but He will never be content merely to placate our passing hungers when our deeper, more profound needs are yet unsatisfied. He came to do more than provide manna in the desert. He came to be the Bread of Life.

Unfortunately, for many of his followers, this talk of spiritual bread was of little interest:

> *From this time many of his disciples turned back and no longer followed him.*

> (John 6:66)

They had seen the signs. They had tasted the evidence. They should have known that God was moving in their midst. Yet somehow, they missed it.

Stomach or Soul?

Fortunately, not all of Jesus' disciples were so blind:

> *"You do not want to leave too, do you?" Jesus asked the Twelve.*
>
> *Simon Peter answered him, "Lord, to whom shall we go? You have the words of eternal life. We believe and know that you are the Holy One of God."*
>
> (John 6:67-69)

Simon Peter and the rest of the twelve, along with others who are not named specifically, saw God where the rest missed His moving.

Simon Peter and the others had already learned to focus on the Provider rather than his provision.

Why? What made them so different? Was it simply that they had a closer walk with Jesus? Perhaps that they had spent more time with him? These are all plausible solutions to the puzzle, but I suspect their intimacy and their time with Jesus were really the result of something else: *Simon Peter and the others had already learned to focus on the Provider rather than His provision.*

In the fifth chapter of Luke we find an interesting story about Jesus' calling of the first disciples. It's a story that many people are familiar with, a story about another miraculous provision:

One day as Jesus was standing by the Lake of Gennesaret with the people crowding around him and listening to the word of God, he saw at the water's edge two boats, left there by the fishermen, who were washing their nets. He got into one of the boats, the one belonging to Simon, and asked him to put out a little from shore. Then he sat down and taught the people from the boat.

When he had finished speaking, he said to Simon, "Put out into deep water, and let down the nets for a catch." Simon answered, "Master, we've worked hard all night and haven't caught anything. But because you say so, I will let down the nets."

When they had done so, they caught such a large number of fish that their nets began to break. So they signaled their partners in the other boat to come and help them, and they came and filled both boats so full that they began to sink. When Simon Peter saw this, he fell at Jesus' knees and said, "Go away from me, Lord; I am a sinful man!" For he and all his companions were astonished at the catch of fish they had taken, and so were James and John, the sons of Zebedee, Simon's partners. Then Jesus said to Simon, "Don't be afraid; from now on you will catch men."

(Luke 5:1-10)

It's a great story and I can't help but wish I could have been there to see it. I can't really imagine how excited Simon Peter and his friends must have been. They were, after all, not what we would call commercial fishermen and this lake wasn't exactly renowned for its massive catches of fish. For these young men, this incredible haul meant that they could feed their families, trade for supplies, maybe even sell some surplus and put a little money away for a rainy day. This was a tremendous provision for them.

It is only when we understand how great a provision this was that we can fully understand how remarkable their response was to Jesus' invitation to come with Him. In his typically understated manner, Luke describes it this way:

So they pulled their boats up on shore, left everything and followed him.

(Luke 5:11)

...as excited as they were about the fish, they were far more excited about Jesus himself.

They left *everything* and followed him. You understand what that includes, right? Not just homes, brothers, sisters, mothers, children

156

and fields (Mark 10:28-30) but also the miraculous catch of fish! Those boats, filled to sinking with God's miraculous provision of fish, were hauled up on the shore and abandoned. Why? Because as excited as they were about the fish, they were far more excited about Jesus himself. So when Jesus called, they answered.

Now, I'm not suggesting that they fully understood the significance of their actions at that moment. I think it quite likely that, at the time, they were simply blown away by the idea that someone like Jesus would want to have anything to do with people like them. After all, they weren't from privilege, power or position. Rabbis typically chose disciples from among the best and the brightest of Israel, from the influential families with connections and prospects.

But these young men had none of that. They had no bright and shining future. Their families had no social or political clout. They were, to put in bluntly, hicks from the sticks. And yet Jesus took notice of them and invited them to become his disciples.

And they said yes. If someone like Jesus was willing to include people like them, they were on board!

And there's the important thing: from the beginning, their focus was on Jesus rather than on what he gave to them. Their focus was on the Provider, not the provision.

To be sure, they probably assumed that anyone who could bring about that miraculous catch of fish could and would continue to provide for them. And they were right, of course. But see, there's a fundamental difference between trusting in the Provider to provide and trusting in the provisions themselves.

For Peter and the rest of the Twelve, Jesus himself was far more important than anything He provided for them miraculously or otherwise. I believe that is why they were able to say, "*Lord, to whom shall we go?*" when so many of the crowd turned away from Jesus. The crowd's eyes were on the provision. The Apostles' eyes were on the Provider.

Gift-getting is a tricky business, maybe even more so than gift-giving. On the one hand, there's a lot of pressure to be excited about the gift itself. But on the other hand, we're supposed to be more grateful *to* the giver than we are *for* the gift. That can be a very tricky line to walk.

Believe me, I know.

Gifts and Givers

When I was in junior in college, I came to the reluctant conclusion that I wasn't walking that line very well. See, a few years earlier, God had given me a gift of music in a rather miraculous fashion (another story for another time) and I had done my best to use it for His glory – at least at first. But music can be a powerful thing, and as doors continued to open for me to "serve" with my gift of music, the music itself took on greater and greater significance. Of course, I have to admit in retrospect that it wasn't *just* about the music – the attention and the minor celebrity were kind of fun too, but I could always justify those. After all, they were only the natural result of the song-writing, singing and worship-leading, all of which were only the natural outgrowth of the gift of music that God Himself had given me. It wasn't like I was seeking those things, so was there really any harm in enjoying them a little?

Over time, however, it became increasingly clear to me that the music – and all that accompanied it – was subtly stealing my focus. I began to hear more and more of that troubling voice in the recesses of my soul asking questions that I didn't really want to answer. Over the course of several months I tried hard to put off that irksome voice, deflecting uncomfortable questions with the facts: I never set out to be a musician…God had given me the gift. I hadn't done things to promote myself…God had opened up the doors. I wasn't looking to get rich or famous…I was going into Christian music (and this was back when Christian music wasn't big business yet). All of that was true. But still the nagging sense that something wasn't right continued to plague me.

It all came to a head during spring break down in Daytona Beach. And just so you know, I wasn't there to party. I had joined a group of Christians who were down there doing evangelism on the beach…really!

One night we all got together for a big rally in a huge tent. There was a great time of worship followed by a speaker. I don't remember who the speaker was or what he said, but I do remember that somewhere in the middle of his message, I felt God call me out of the tent and onto the beach. I made my way out of the packed assembly and out to the deserted shore...and started walking. Somewhere down the beach I had one of those rare moments (for me at least) where I heard the Voice clearly. And this is what He said to me: *How important is this music stuff to you?*

Startled by the stark clarity of it, I stopped there on the beach, expecting more...but I didn't hear anything else. So, I tried a probing question: "What do you mean, Lord? It has to be important, doesn't it? You gave it to me!"

And God said: nothing. Absolutely nothing.

I sat down on that empty beach and stared out at the dark sea. I was waiting, I suppose, for an answer, but the more I waited the more I realized *He* was still waiting for *my* answer.

I wasn't entirely sure what to say. I still felt that the fact that God had given me this gift and the opportunities that came with it somehow made the gift itself worthy of attention. I sincerely felt that to say "the music isn't important at all" would somehow convey a lack of gratitude.

I sat there for a long time until, very gradually, an answer began to take shape. I considered this answer very carefully and finally concluded that this was the only answer that could be given.

I remember sighing, looking up and saying softly, "Not as important as You, Lord."

There was no angelic chorus that broke over me that night. No parting of the heavens and a glimpse of a smiling God peering down at me. God didn't even bother to say anything else – not a "good answer" or even an "attaboy!" What happened instead was a clear sense that something like tension suddenly bled from the night around me, though I suppose it was only a projection of a release in my soul.

Though there was no doubt that I had given the right answer, an answer I genuinely believed, there was still the problem of what to do with it. Abraham had a boy to put on an altar. Peter had a boat full of fish to leave on a shore. But how was I supposed to put my "Not as important as You, Lord" into practice?

Well, long story short(er), I made a phone call when I got back from Daytona Beach that spring. It was a call to Youth With A Mission, a group I was scheduled to go to Eastern Europe with that summer. The plan had been to be a guitarist/singer with a band that was going to do evangelism in Bulgaria, but I called them and asked if I could go along as a sound engineer instead. And that's what I did. That was my altar. That was my boat full of fish left on the shore. That was the way I put feet to my "Not as important as You, Lord" answer.

It was an interesting summer. God did more in and through me that summer than I can possibly sum up here in a few paragraphs at the conclusion of this chapter. I will tell you this, though: like Abraham, I got my sacrifice back. Like Peter, I received far more than I left behind. I ended up back on stage as a guitarist and singer when some rather bizarre circumstances forced me to it that summer. I made a decision to trust the Provider rather than the provision and I ended up with both.

It doesn't always work that way. Sometimes we turn away from a provision and to the Provider and never see that particular provision again. I've had some of those experiences over the years, too. But you know what? I've never missed them. And I've never lacked for anything I really needed. That's the advantage of sticking close to the Provider...He, well, *provides*.

What's Your Basket?

I don't know what basketful of provision might be weighing you down right now because you've got too tight a hold on it. I don't know what boat you might have your hand glued to at the moment. I don't know what provision might be taking your eyes off the Provider.

> When our focus is on the gift rather than the Giver, we are in danger of missing God move.

Understand, I'm not saying the gifts are bad. He's a very good Giver, after all. It's just that no gift He's ever given can possibly compare to the Giver Himself. So while I don't know what particular gift you might be struggling with at this moment in

162

your life, I do know this: when our focus is on the gift rather than the Giver, we are in danger of missing God move.

And no gift is worth that.

Questions for Discussion

1. *How would you explain the difference between joy and happiness?*

2. *Can you think of a time that difficult circumstances have made it hard for you to see what God was doing?*

3. *Can you think of a time that pleasant circumstances have made it hard for you to see what God was doing?*

4. *Why do you think we are prone to focus on God's gifts rather than on Him as the Giver?*

5. *Do you have a "basket" of God's provision right now that you might be holding onto too tightly?*

Chapter 6

Conflicted Hearts

Palm Sunday.

Chances are, if you grew up in church at all, you remember this as the Sunday little kids paraded through the worship services waving palm branches – not exactly the height of creativity, but at least it's a tradition that makes sense, right?

The palm branches aren't some esoteric symbol; they are literal reminders of the palm branches that some of Jesus' followers laid on the road in front of him as he made his way into Jerusalem during what we call his "Triumphal Entry" (John 12:13). This occurred, of course, on the week before he was crucified, which makes "triumphant" a somewhat ironic way to describe this journey.

Tragic Triumph

In spite of the way this visit to Jerusalem turned out, there are good reasons to call his entrance *triumphant*. There were, after all, several unique aspects to it.

First, this is the only time we know of that Jesus ever rode anywhere. Perhaps some of our Christmas nativity scenes are right and his mother, Mary, took a donkey to Bethlehem, allowing Jesus to catch a ride in utero. Other than that slim possibility, however, we don't know of any time that Jesus ever rode an animal anywhere. Whenever we see Jesus going from place to place in the Gospels, he was walking. I suppose we must admit that he sometimes rode in a boat, but even out on water he sometimes preferred to walk!

But for this entrance into Jerusalem, Jesus chose to enter on a previously unridden colt and its mother (Mat 21:2-7, Luke 19:29-34[21]). While there are some debates about exactly what his choice of transportation signified, the overall consensus is clear: this was a kingly act. The point is simply that riding an animal into a city was something

---

[21] Matthew speaks of both animals (the colt and its mother), whereas Luke only speaks of the colt. Though the reason for this is not entirely clear, this is not a contradiction. Luke has not denied that the mother donkey was present – he has simply focused on the unridden colt.

that common people didn't do. Jesus riding instead of walking hinted to his disciples that he was finally ready to make a public declaration of himself as God's anointed king.

This entry was also triumphant because Jesus took possession of his transportation in an interesting way that demonstrated his authority as king. In the original Greek of both Mathew and Luke, Jesus is reported to have told his disciples to tell the animals' owners "the Lord has need of them." Most English versions render this simply as "the Lord needs them," but the original wording is significantly more pointed, appearing to state that Jesus thought of the donkeys as his property. Since he didn't own any donkeys, this only makes sense if we understand that Jesus was announcing himself as king so that everything in Israel belonged to him in a royal sense.

Third, this entry into Jerusalem was triumphant because Jesus accepted honor from his followers in a way that he hadn't previously. As Luke tells it:

> *When he came near the place where the road goes down the Mount of Olives, the whole crowd of disciples began joyfully to praise God in loud voices for all the miracles they had seen: "Blessed is the king who comes in the name of the Lord!" "Peace in heaven and glory in the highest!"*

> (Luke 19:37-38)

Earlier in his ministry, Jesus often silenced people (and demons) who recognized him for who he was. So pronounced was this tendency that scholars have even come up with a name for it: the Messianic Secret. It appears that Jesus did not want public recognition too early, perhaps knowing that it would have accelerated his journey to the cross before he had completed other things he had come to do. In any event, this day outside of Jerusalem was different. Whereas before he had tried to minimize public recognition, now he accepted and even encouraged it, both by his actions and by his words:

> *Some of the Pharisees in the crowd said to Jesus, "Teacher, rebuke your disciples!"*
>
> *"I tell you," he replied, "if they keep quiet, the stones will cry out."*

> (Luke 19:39-40)

It is here, with the Pharisees' concern, that we get our first hint that the Triumphal Entry was not a universally welcomed event.

We often picture this scene as though thousands upon thousands of adoring pilgrims danced and sang around Jesus as he rode towards the city gates. In reality, his arrival received a mixed reaction. To be sure, Matthew does talk about "the crowds that went ahead of him" (Mat 21:9), but Luke clarifies that this was a "crowd of disciples" (Luke 19:37), and as we have already seen, this was a crowd that had been significantly reduced.

170

And, quite obviously, not everyone was happy to see Jesus coming towards Jerusalem. The Pharisees in particular were less than ecstatic.

Cause for Concern

Their concern was not without some justification. Jesus' entry into Jerusalem coincided with the arrival of a multitude of pilgrims coming to the Holy City for the Passover Feast. Rome, always on the lookout for anything that hinted at rebellion, would have been keeping a careful eye on all these arriving visitors. For one pilgrim to arrive riding an animal that likely symbolized royalty, greeted by a crowd (however small it might have been) singing his praises and saying, "Blessed is the king who comes in the name of the Lord!"...well, you can see why that might have caught their interest.

So perhaps the Pharisees' concern was nothing more than a sincere desire not to stir up the Roman soldiers' suspicion and, potentially, wrath. Understandable or not, however, the Pharisees' objection to the honor Jesus was receiving points to another issue, one which has been our primary concern throughout this book: why couldn't they see what the disciples saw? Why didn't they realize who Jesus was or what God was doing?

The fact is, the central difference between the crowd of disciples and the representatives of the Pharisees here on the road was that the disciples saw God moving...and the Pharisees missed it.

But why? What kept them from seeing God move?

All the Usual Suspects

There are actually several candidates here. One of them, so often associated with the Pharisees, is *hypocrisy*. Perhaps the issue was that while they said they served God, in actuality it was themselves that they were most interested in. This is possible, but as we saw earlier, this is probably an overly uncharitable view of the Pharisees. Certainly hypocrisy was a major issue in their camp, one Jesus called them out on, but there was some division of opinion among the Pharisees regarding whether or not Jesus was God's servant. So while hypocrisy might have been a contributor to the problem, there's probably more going on here than that.

The fear of what might be clouds our ability to see what is really happening right before us.

Another option to explain the Pharisees' failure to see God moving here is *fear*. Perhaps they were simply so afraid of what the Romans might do if a rebellion appeared to be brewing, that they were unable to see the bigger picture. Fear often has that effect on us. This fear can emerge from many things, several of which we discussed in the chapter called "When Kingdoms Collide." But regardless of what precisely we are afraid of, the result is the same: the fear of what might be clouds our ability to see what is really happening right before us. It is quite likely that the Pharisees' fear of what the Romans *might* have done significantly affected their ability to see what God *was* doing at that very moment.

Perhaps another contributor to their blindness was what I sometimes call a *crippling nostalgia*. The Pharisees, perhaps more than any other group in Israel in those days, were prone to looking backwards rather than forwards. They tended to look at how God had moved in the past and assume that when He moved again it would be in precisely the same way.

But this Jesus was something new. He knew the Scriptures, sure, but he seemed terribly irreverent about them, at least from the Pharisees' perspective. He wouldn't obey the rules about the Sabbath they had set up to make sure people were safely pious. He hung out with people whose very existence threatened to pollute their rigid understanding of holiness. This Jesus was, in short, a radical...and the Pharisees didn't like radicals. They wanted a return to the good old days when God had moved in ways that were both comfortable and familiar.

In short, the Pharisees were so fixated on how God had moved in the past that they couldn't see what He was doing now. That's what I mean by a *crippling nostalgia*: a fixation on the past that keeps us from moving forward.

Too many of our churches today struggle to see God moving for the same reason. I cannot tell you how many churches I have visited over the years that are fixated on what God has done in the past, yet seem to be blind to what God is doing now. It's terribly depressing.

I'm not saying there is no value in remembering the past, especially when it is a past in which God's faithfulness is so evident. On the contrary, I believe there is great value in erecting monuments that look to the past in order to find confidence for the future. But when a place is filled with reminders of the past that stop at "remember when?" and do not challenge us to boldly trust ourselves to that same God in an as-yet unknown future, that place is not so much a monument as it is a *mausoleum*. Far, far too many of our churches today are more like mausoleums than monuments, and it is often a crippling nostalgia that makes them such.

All of these reasons may have contributed to the Pharisees' inability to see God moving as Jesus entered Jerusalem, but I believe the Gospel writers explicitly identify another issue at play.

Stony Silence

The first hint of this real issue is actually contained in the statement that Jesus made to the effect that if the people did not welcome him as king then "the stones will cry out."

This is often taken to mean that if human beings did not acknowledge Jesus' true identity, then nature itself would bear witness. However, while there are plenty of poetic references in Scripture to the creation testifying to God's glory, this business about stones crying out was more likely a pointed citation of a passage from the book of Habakkuk:

> *"Woe to him who builds his realm by unjust gain to set his nest on high, to escape the clutches of ruin! You have plotted the ruin of many peoples, shaming your own house and forfeiting your life. <u>The stones of the</u>*

wall will cry out, and the beams of the woodwork will echo it, "Woe to him who builds a city with bloodshed and establishes a town by injustice!"[22]

(Habakkuk 2:9-12)

Rather than being a reference to a cry of exaltation, Jesus was likely prophesying that the stones of Jerusalem would cry out in judgment. This interpretation is made nearly certain by what happens next in Luke's account:

As he approached Jerusalem and saw the city, he wept over it and said, "If you, even you, had only known on this day what would bring you peace – but now it is hidden from your eyes. The days will come upon you when your enemies will build an embankment against you and encircle you and hem you in on every side. They will dash you to the ground, you and the children within your walls. They will not leave one stone on another, because you did not recognize the time of God's coming to you."

(Luke 19:41-44)

---

[22] I have modified the New International Version slightly on this final word. The NIV renders the Hebrew term here (*avlah*) as "crime" and the New American Standard as "violence." Both terms are perfectly serviceable translations, but it is my opinion that the *avlah* was used here to speak more of someone being denied what is just and right than of criminal activity per se, hence my substitution of "injustice."

When these words of Jesus are considered, it seems clear that he was not speaking of inanimate stones rendering worship but of broken walls testifying to guilt. Jesus' prophecy was fulfilled in 70 A.D. when the armies of Rome destroyed Jerusalem and literally left "not one stone on another."

And what was the cause of this judgment that was passed upon the city of Jerusalem and so many of its inhabitants? *"You did not recognize the time of God's coming to you"* (Luke 19:44).

But this drives us again to ask the all-important question of what kept them from seeing God move? Why did they miss it?

Into the Robbers' Den

Jesus' quotation of Habakkuk provides an important insight. In Habakkuk 2, the reason for the judgment which the stones of the walls passed upon their inhabitants was quite clear: *"Woe to him who builds a city with bloodshed and establishes a town by injustice!"* (Hab 2:12).

But what injustice was Jesus referring to when he called attention to this well-known passage from Habakkuk? The answer lies in the events that follow in Luke's account:

> *Then he entered the temple area and began driving out those who were selling. "It is written," he said to them, "'My house will be a house of prayer'; but you have made it 'a den of robbers.'"*

176

Though this speech by Jesus was very brief, it was what we might call "theologically loaded." It doesn't take any special knowledge or training to feel the impact of this accusation when Jesus called the place intended to be a "house of prayer" a "den of robbers." That blunt and caustic turn of phrase does an excellent job of conveying Jesus' frustration. But what precisely was the cause of his frustration or – dare we say it? – His anger?

We often assume that Jesus was upset with the commercialism of it all: people were engaged in the mundane act of buying and selling in a place that was supposed to be dedicated to more transcendent pursuits: to worship and prayer and contemplation of God and His will for His people. I've been in more than one church that has made it a policy to prohibit selling anything on church grounds precisely because that is what they assume Jesus was preaching against here.

But of course, Luke didn't say Jesus was upset they had turned the Temple into a *marketplace*,[23] he said they had

---

[23] Interestingly, John recounts that Jesus once rebuked a group of money-changers for turning "my Father's house into a market!" (John 2:16). Moreover, this rebuke was given while Jesus was "cleansing" the Temple. Scholars are divided on whether John was describing the same temple cleansing that the Synoptic Gospels (Matthew/Mark/Luke) describe or another, additional cleansing. While there are reasons to think that there might have been two separate Temple cleansings (not the least of which is the fact that John places his cleansing at the beginning rather than the end of Jesus' ministry), the details of the various accounts are so similar in most respects that I find a the two-cleansing theory unconvincing. It seems likely to me that both John

turned it into a *"den of robbers."* Because of this, some readers assume that there was cheating going on among the merchants and they were kicked out because of their corruption. Perhaps they were overcharging for the sacrifices they sold or using unfair exchange rates when converting the pilgrims' Roman coins into the half-shekel required for the Temple tax. The problem with this view is that, while it's easy to imagine such a thing going on, nothing to that effect is actually said here. And besides, Jesus didn't call them "cheats" or "thieves" but "robbers."

To most English speakers, the word "robber" may seem synonymous with "thief" or "cheat," but it actually has a slightly different meaning. A "thief" is someone who steals, but a "robber" is someone who takes by force. Even today, our legal system distinguishes between theft and robbery, specifying that robbery always entails a form of violence or threat of violence.

The same distinction is present in the original languages of Scripture as well. The Greek term translated as "robbers" in Luke 19:46 is *lēstēs*. It's the same term used in Mat 26:55 when Jesus asked those who came to arrest him,

---

and the Synoptic are describing the same event and that differences such as "market" vs. "den of robbers" exist because the Synoptics and John focused on different things Jesus said during the event. In other words, Jesus said more than what John reports and more than what the Synoptics report, making it likely that Jesus said both "you've turned my Father's house into a market" and "you've turned the house of prayer into a den of robbers." There is nothing inherently contradictory about these two different statements if they are separate indictments. For his purposes, John wanted to highlight the "market" business and the Synoptics wanted to highlight the "den of robbers" accusation.

"Have you come out with swords and clubs to arrest me as you would against a <u>robber</u>?"[24] It's also the same term used in John 18:40 to describe Barabbas (the man released instead of Jesus) as a man of violence.

The point is that cheating pilgrims out of money by overcharging or by unfair exchange rates would have been *theft*, certainly, but it wouldn't have been *robbery* of the sort that Jesus seems to have been implying. Whatever Jesus was upset about, it seems to have been more serious than just unfair business practices.

But the biggest problem with thinking that Jesus was upset with the commercialism – or even with corrupt commercialism – is simply that the merchants and moneychangers were all doing something that was absolutely necessary. Money-changing was needed because the Temple tax could only be made with a coin that was not in wide-spread circulation. And Temple regulations required that things needed for the sacrifices be made available to pilgrims, especially for those who had to travel great distances to get to the Temple. So both the money-changers and the merchants had legitimate reasons for doing what they were doing.

So why was Jesus so upset?

---

[24] New American Standard. The NIV translates *lēstēs* here as "leading a rebellion." The term appears to have had multiple uses in the first century, both as a robber and as a rebel; note, however, that both involved violence.

For All Nations

The reason for Jesus' anger is revealed in two additional Old Testament passages, both of which Jesus cited here. Just as the earlier short quote from Habakkuk was intended to remind his listeners of a familiar prophetic judgment that would have been clear to anyone familiar with the passage he was pointing to, Jesus here was drawing their attention to indictments made by the prophets Isaiah and Jeremiah.

When he called the Temple a "house of prayer," Jesus was calling his listeners to remember – and to reflect on – the following words from Isaiah:

> *This is what the LORD says: "Maintain justice and do what is right, for my salvation is close at hand and my righteousness will soon be revealed. Blessed is the man who does this, the man who holds it fast, who keeps the Sabbath without desecrating it, and keeps his hand from doing any evil."*
>
> *Let no foreigner who has bound himself to the LORD say, "The LORD will surely exclude me from his people." And let not any eunuch complain, "I am only a dry tree."*
>
> *For this is what the LORD says: "To the eunuchs who keep my Sabbaths, who choose what pleases me and hold fast to my covenant – to them I will give within my temple and its walls a memorial and a name*

better than sons and daughters; I will give them an everlasting name that will not be cut off. And foreigners who bind themselves to the LORD to serve him, to love the name of the LORD, and to worship him, all who keep the Sabbath without desecrating it and who hold fast to my covenant – these I will bring to my holy mountain and give them joy in my house of prayer. Their burnt offerings and sacrifices will be accepted on my altar; for my house will be called a house of prayer for all nations."

(Isaiah 56:1-7)

There are three things to pay special attention to here. First, notice that this passage of Isaiah has more than a passing concern for the plight of the "foreigner" and the "eunuch," both of which were classes of people normally excluded from worship at the Temple in first century Israel. Second, notice that God here says that both foreigners and eunuchs who obey His commands will have an "everlasting name," indicating that they will receive the same salvation promised to Israel. Third, notice that the phrase "house of prayer" which Jesus quoted is actually part of a larger phrase: "a house of prayer for all nations." Clearly this portion of Isaiah reveals that God loves all peoples of the world and not just the blood descendants of Abraham.

Similarly, when Jesus used the phrase "den of robbers," he was calling his listeners to remember – and to reflect on – the following words from Jeremiah:

This is the word that came to Jeremiah from the LORD:

Stand at the gate of the LORD's house and there proclaim this message:

Hear the word of the LORD, all you people of Judah who come through these gates to worship the LORD. This is what the LORD Almighty, the God of Israel, says: "Reform your ways and your actions, and I will let you live in this place. Do not trust in deceptive words and say, 'This is the temple of the LORD, the temple of the LORD, the temple of the LORD!'"

"If you really change your ways and your actions and deal with each other justly, if you do not oppress the alien, the fatherless or the widow and do not shed innocent blood in this place, and if you do not follow other gods to your own harm, then I will let you live in this place, in the land I gave your forefathers for ever and ever. But look, you are trusting in deceptive words that are worthless."

"Will you steal and murder, commit adultery and perjury, burn incense to Baal

and follow other gods you have not known,
and then come and stand before me in this
house, which bears my Name, and say, 'We
are safe' – safe to do all these detestable
things?"

"Has this house, which bears my Name,
become a den of robbers to you? But I have
been watching!" declares the LORD.

(Jeremiah 7:1-11)

As you read that passage, you may have noticed that it contained some themes that are very similar to the passage from Isaiah we looked at above. One thing that may have stood out particularly was the fact that God defined justice in this context as not oppressing the alien/foreigner (as well as the fatherless and the widow). As in the Isaiah passage, God seems to be revealing His concern here for the Gentiles (a word used to refer to non-Jewish people). But going beyond just revealing God's love for the Gentiles, this passage also reveals that God was deeply concerned with how the people of Israel treated the Gentiles.

Between these two Old Testament passages, we see that God wanted the Gentiles to know Him and to be able to worship Him, to be drawn into relationship with Him that would be to their blessing. This should have come as no surprise to anyone. As far back as Abraham, the first of God's people, God had specifically stated that His blessing of the Hebrews had a larger purpose:

"I will make you into a great nation and I will bless you; I will make your name great, and you will be a blessing. I will bless those who bless you, and whoever curses you I will curse; and all peoples on earth will be blessed through you."

(Genesis 12:2-3)

It was clearly God's intention from the very beginning that His blessing of Israel would reverberate out to all people. In many ways, Jesus was the clearest example of this. Jesus was, of course, a Jew, descended from Abraham, and he died to make salvation available to "those who were far away and those who were near" (Eph 2:17). In that passage from Ephesians, "those who were near" was a euphemism for the Jews and "those who were far away" was a euphemism for the Gentiles. Through Jesus, all peoples on earth have been blessed, fulfilling God's promise to Abraham all those millennia ago.

But here's the thing: Jesus was the *greatest* fulfillment of God's promise, but he was not the *first* or *only* fulfillment. God had already made other provisions for blessing the Gentiles. One of the ways God had done that was to allow Gentiles to worship at the great Jewish Temple in Jerusalem.

In Jesus' day, there were quite a few Gentiles who longed to serve and obey the God of Abraham, Isaac and Jacob. They were called "God-fearers" and they were allowed into the Temple to worship. However, because they were not

184

circumcised and thus were considered perpetually unclean, they were not allowed past the Outer Court of the Temple. Because of this restriction, the Outer Court is sometimes called the "Court of the Gentiles" today, though there is no evidence that it was ever called this in ancient times.

The point of this is simply that there was a place set up in the Temple for the foreigner and the alien to worship God; a place where they could contemplate His glory, give thanks for His loving-kindness, praise His faithfulness and humbly seek His presence.

And guess where the money-changers and sacrifice-sellers had set up shop?

That's right. They were conducting their business in the Outer Court.

Imagine trying to worship while people around you are hawking their wares. Worse, imagine trying to worship when the wares they're hawking were live animals! How much contemplation could you do while lambs bleated and goats brayed? How easy would it be to still your soul while money-changers and merchants competed for your attention?

"I will give you a great deal, my friend!"

"You are my first customer of the day!"

"I have the most spotless lambs in Jerusalem! Buy one from me today and I will throw in a free dove...okay, okay, make it two doves!"

You get the point. It would be virtually impossible to engage in authentic worship under such circumstances, yet this is precisely what the Gentile God-fearers faced. Their opportunity to worship the God of Abraham, Isaac and Jacob was being forcibly torn from them in a cacophony of commercialism.

But let's be clear, it wasn't the commercialism itself that was the problem, it was where it was taking place. That place which was supposed to be a "house of prayer for all nations" had been turned into a "den of violent ones." The violence was metaphorical, of course, but it was no less heinous for that fact. God longed to provide sanctuary for all who would come, even for the uncircumcised Gentiles, but this sanctuary was being denied them.

Of course, the real issue wasn't just that the merchants and money-lenders had been allowed to conduct their business in the Outer Court. The real issue was *why* they had been allowed to do so: because who cared what happened in the Outer Court? Who cared if the Gentiles didn't have a good place to worship? Who cared if the foreigner and the alien were unable to focus on the God of Abraham? It's not like the Jews were affected. Pious Jewish men and even women had other places they could go in the Temple for undisturbed worship. So who cared if the Outer Court was a madhouse?

Who cared? God did.

Stony Hearts

But the Pharisees didn't care, at least not as a whole group. They didn't care about the Gentiles and their opportunity to worship, to learn, to understand. They had forgotten God's promise to Abraham: *"I will bless those who bless you...and all peoples on earth will be blessed through you."*

And that is why the Pharisees didn't see God moving as Jesus entered Jerusalem. That is why they were unable to "recognize the time of God's coming to you." Not because they were afraid or hypocritical or caught in a crippling nostalgia, though these may all have been present as well. No, the Pharisees there on the road missed God moving that day because they didn't care about what God cared about. Their hearts did not beat with His.

> ...when we are callous to the things that cause Him the greatest grief, we will miss God move...

When our hearts don't beat with God's...when we are callous to the very things that cause Him the greatest grief, we will miss God move simply because we won't even be looking in the right direction.

I believe the Pharisees were unable to see God moving simply because they didn't care about what He cared about. This was something that had been a cause of conflict throughout Jesus' ministry. The Pharisees were upset when Jesus healed on the Sabbath because they didn't care about the suffering. The Pharisees were upset when Jesus spent time with "sinners" because they didn't care about the lost. They simply didn't care about what Jesus cared about and so they were unable to see what God was doing in and through him.

When we don't care about what God cares about, we will miss Him moving.

Consider the following statements of what God cares about:

> *For I desire mercy, not sacrifice, and acknowledgment of God rather than burnt offerings.*
>
> (Hosea 6:6)

> *Jesus replied: "'Love the Lord your God with all your heart and with all your soul and with all your mind.' This is the first and greatest commandment. And the second is like it: 'Love your neighbor as yourself.' All the Law and the Prophets hang on these two commandments."*
>
> (Matthew 22:37-40)

> *If anyone considers himself religious and yet does not keep a tight rein on his tongue, he deceives himself and his religion is worthless. Religion that God our Father accepts as pure and faultless is this: to look after orphans and widows in their distress and to keep oneself from being polluted by the world.*
>
> (James 1:26-27)

If I speak in the tongues of men and of angles, but have not love, I am only a resounding gong or a clanging cymbal. If I have the gift of prophecy and can fathom all mysteries and all knowledge, and if I have a faith that can move mountains, but have not love, I am nothing. If I give all I possess to the poor and surrender my body to the flames, but have not love, I gain nothing.

(1 Corinthians 13:1-3)

Obviously this list is by no means exhaustive, but it is worth a moment of our time to ask ourselves if we care about the sorts of things that God says matter so much to Him.

If your honest answer is "not really," then perhaps instead of asking God to let you see Him move, what you need to be asking is for Him to stir your heart so that it beats and breaks with His. Because only then will you be in a position to see Him move.

Misplaced Priorities

Unfortunately, there is a corollary to this principle that is also true: we can miss God move because we care too much about the wrong things, things that God really doesn't give all that much thought to.

For the Pharisees, the Sabbath rules were all-important. They couldn't celebrate with a blind man who could suddenly see…all because his healing took place on a day – and in a way – that offended their far-more-important rules about how to keep the Sabbath holy. They couldn't marvel at a woman's obvious transformation in Jesus' presence because they were too fixated on what she had been and how her presence might reflect on them now.

When we care too much about the wrong things, we are just as much in danger of missing God move as when we don't care at all about the things that matter to Him. Caring too much about the wrong things means that not only are we not looking where we should be looking but that, instead, all of our attention is somewhere else entirely.

I once served as a youth pastor at a church that backed up to the local high school. It was an older, traditional church whose biggest step of faith in many years was hiring a very young youth pastor from outside the denomination to "keep the kids interested."

By the grace of God, during my time there, our church became the place to hang out after school for a lot of teenagers. I worked hard to make students feel welcome and wanted. My office was always open and I could usually be counted on for an impromptu game of church darts, extreme hide & seek (don't ask) or sand volleyball. Over time, this translated into deep relationships, trust, heartfelt sharing, salvation experiences, profound discipleship and more. The youth ministry grew dramatically.

But not everyone was happy about that. I started getting notes of complaint – usually anonymous Post-It notes that complained about the noise and the fact that so many of the kids' parents "don't go to this church." My all-time favorite note (sarcasm) was this: "All these kids are wearing a track in the carpet from the back door to your office. Please tell them to take alternate routes."

I hope those words break your heart. I know they broke mine. Students, many of them with no other church experience at all, were literally wearing a track in the carpet to the youth pastor's office…and someone thought that was a bad thing.

Ironically, that note was one of the ways that I saw God moving…moving me out of that church, that is. It was a difficult thing to realize because I loved those kids and loved what God had done there. But it was also becoming painfully clear that a sustained ministry there would have killed me. Too many – not all, but far, far too many – of them were completely blind to God moving because they were more concerned about the carpets than the kids. They were so fixated on things that don't matter to God at all that they couldn't see what did.

Heartbeats

God's heart is the drum that must order the dance of our lives. When our hearts beat with His, we cannot help but fall into step with Him and see the myriad of ways that He is moving in our midst. But when our hearts fall out of sync with His, we may be so deafened

> God's heart is the drum that must order the dance of our lives.

by the cacophony that results that we will be unable to hear His call or see His moving.

We can miss what God is doing around us because we don't care about the things that matter to Him...or because we care too much about the things that don't. Either way, though, our off-kilter passions can keep us from seeing what we so desperately long to see: God moving in our midst.

As a worship leader, I find that if I'm not careful and deliberate, I can easily end up off on my own, out of sync with the groove the rest of the team is following. Sticking with the beat laid down by the drummer sometimes takes more effort than I would like. You would think it wouldn't take any effort at all. How could you ever lose track of the pounding of a kick drum at your back?

But the reality is that it's not hard at all to lose focus and become so fixated on what I'm doing that I lose track of everything else. When that happens, there is only one solution: start listening again. I have to be deliberate about tuning in to what the drums are doing and finding my proper place. When that happens, there's a magical moment when what I'm playing or singing suddenly clicks into place with the rest of the sonic landscape and all is right with the world.

It's like that with God. You might be in a place where your heart doesn't beat with His, but you can fix that...or I should say God can fix that if only you will let Him. The Holy Spirit in you is straining against the bounds of this discord, longing to bring you back into sync with the Divine rhythm. All you have to do is listen.

Questions for Discussion

1. *Can you relate to the Pharisees' fears that what Jesus was doing would spark conflict with their earthly obligations? Why or why not?*

2. *Make a list of at least 10 things that you know God cares about deeply. Then indicate the degree to which each of these is something you care about.*

God cares about...	This matters to me...		
	Not at All	Just a Little	Quite a Lot

3. Now, make a list of at least 10 things that you care about deeply. Don't over-spiritualize this. Just be honest about what matters to you most right now. When you're finished, decide how much each of these things matters to God.

	This matters to God...		
I care about...	Not at All	Just a Little	Quite a Lot

4. As you consider these two lists, where do you see the greatest disconnect between your priorities and God's?

5. *Is there anything holding you back from listening to God's heartbeat and getting in sync with it? If so, what would it take to get past that obstacle?*

About The Author

From Jr. High retreats to international pastor conferences and everything in between, Craig speaks to thousands of people around the world every year. With deep, life-changing biblical teaching, relevant storytelling and engaging humor, Craig bridges the gap between the head and the heart, challenging audiences of all ages. Craig is a veteran pastor as well as a respected Christian scholar, so he not only brings solid Bible teaching but also a shepherd's heart to make the Truth understandable and relevant to modern audiences.

Craig divides his professional time between speaking, writing, scholarly pursuits, serving as an elder, teaching pastor and worship leader in his home church and leading the Shepherd Project, an international non-profit Christian equipping ministry.

To inquire about having Craig speak at an event, please contact:

Shepherd Project Ministries
www.shepherdproject.com
1.800.253.1869
info@shepherdproject.com